21世纪商务英语系列教材

国际商务礼仪
英文教程

主　编　张　宇（东北师范大学）
　　　　艾天姿（浙江工业大学）
副主编　华裕涛（东北林业大学）
　　　　马宏梅（东北师范大学）
　　　　任　佳（吉林大学）
　　　　白华英（东北师范大学）
　　　　张　宁（东北师范大学）
编　者　古力斯旦木·哈德尔艾山（伊犁师范学院）
　　　　蒋　菲（东北师范大学）
　　　　王金鹤（大连外国语学院）
　　　　王金阳（辽宁大学）
　　　　常　晶（东北师范大学）
　　　　彭　微
　　　　卢　丹（东北师范大学）
　　　　宋薇薇（东北师范大学）

U0362609

北京大学出版社
PEKING UNIVERSITY PRESS

图书在版编目(CIP)数据

国际商务礼仪英文教程 /张宇,艾天姿主编. —北京:北京大学出版社,2010.7
(21世纪商务英语系列教材)
ISBN 978-7-301-16108-1

Ⅰ.国… Ⅱ.①张…②艾… Ⅲ.商务—礼仪—英语—高等学校—教材 Ⅳ.H31

中国版本图书馆 CIP 数据核字(2009)第 208431 号

书　　　　名:**国际商务礼仪英文教程**
著作责任者:张　宇　艾天资　主编
责 任 编 辑:李　颖
标 准 书 号:ISBN 978-7-301-16108-1/H·2360
出 版 发 行:北京大学出版社
地　　　　址:北京市海淀区成府路 205 号　100871
网　　　　址:http://www.pup.cn
电　　　　话:邮购部 62752015　发行部 62750672　编辑部 62767315　出版部 62754962
电 子 邮 箱:evalee1770@sina.com
印 　刷 　者:北京鑫海金澳胶印有限公司
经 　销 　者:新华书店
　　　　　　787 毫米×1092 毫米　16 开本　10.5 印张　260 千字
　　　　　　2010 年 7 月第 1 版　2023 年 4 月第 13 次印刷
定　　　　价:24.00 元

序

2009年秋季学期伊始，张宇拿着《国际商务礼仪英文教程》走进我的办公室，希望我为她的大作写序。礼仪不是我研究的领域，不敢贸然落笔。但这位年轻同事的上进心使我不能拒绝她的要求。第一次接触她是在新疆伊犁师范学院。她当时受东北师范大学派遣在那执行教育部学科援疆计划，工作表现出色，深受师生欢迎。我当时作为对口支援工作负责人，发自内心地感谢张宇等一批教师很好地完成了这项意义深远的工作。有过这段经历，我只好努力满足她的要求，写点儿我的读后感。再说，年已花甲的老教师看到青年同事如此上进也格外高兴，助他们成功是我们的幸事。

礼节或礼仪是"规定社会行为和职业行为准则的习俗和体系"（《不列颠百科全书》（中译本）第6页）。违反礼节不至于受到制裁，但会受到责难或冷遇。这是礼节的社会属性使然，一个人独处可能无需顾及礼节（但也要慎独），两个人或众人在一起则必须遵守礼节。即使亲密无间的夫妻之间也提倡相敬如宾。可见礼节和礼仪的实质在于处理好人际关系。社会不是简单的个体集合，而是由不同角色的社会人构成的整体。有人群就势必有礼节，古今中外概莫能外。

在中国，礼仪源于上古时期的祭祀文化。我们的祖先在崇拜自然神，崇拜先辈的祭祀活动中形成了中华民族早期的礼仪（见付亚庶著《中国上古祭祀文化》（第二版），高等教育出版社，2005）。在西方，"宫廷是礼节的发源地，它以君主为中心，把各种行为的细节逐步向各个阶层传播"（《不列颠百科全书》（中译本）第6页）。在现代社会，礼仪不只是达官贵人必须注意的事，也是平民百姓应该注意的事。人们在求职面试、商务谈判、相亲访友、参会发言等各种各样的活动中都必须讲究礼节，在平等互动中表现出对对方的尊重。个人的修养见于一言一行，事情的成败往往在于当事人是否举止得体，言辞得当。

认识礼仪的社会性和普遍性还不够，还要知道它的文化性或民族性。不同的文化在长期沿革过程中形成了各自的礼仪。从事跨文化交流活动必须强化文化差异意识。在经济一体化的背景下国际商务活动越来越频繁，用英语进行国际商务活动自然需要懂得英语国家的礼仪。《国际商务礼仪英文教程》的实用价值显而易见。

礼仪有多种多样的表达方式，包括语言文字、着装、举止、摆设，等等。《国际商务礼仪英文教程》由九章构成，涵盖了国际商务活动礼仪的方方面面，内容丰富多彩，文字浅显易懂，是一本适于经贸类专业学生学习英语的好教材。相信此书的出版会使众多青年学生受益。

杨忠

于东北师范大学外国语学院
2009 年 9 月 27 日

前　言

中国的俗语说"礼多人不怪",意思是,在交往中以礼待人不会令人反感。事实上,以礼待人不止不会招致他人反感,而且能够帮助我们得到他人的欢迎和礼遇。

我们在交往中要接触形形色色的人,人们对于"礼"的理解又不尽相同,"失礼"也就在所难免,待人接物"彬彬有礼"也就成了一种挑战。尤其是在全球化程度日益加深的今天,在国际商务活动中,当交际的双方使用不同的语言、具有不同的文化背景时,加深双方在基本礼仪常识方面的了解和理解,消除礼仪差异造成的交际障碍,提高交际的有效性,是成功的跨文化交际的关键。

本书从服饰容貌、见面问候、拜访接待、西式宴请、面试礼仪、办公室礼仪、电话礼仪、书信礼仪等方面入手,介绍跨文化交际中的基本礼仪常识,旨在为全球化生活、学习和工作环境中的交际者提供基本的行为指引。

国际礼仪存在的意义在于它能够被交际者普遍接受,不问出处,不分国籍。不同的国家和文化固然赋予了礼仪不同的内涵,然而成功的跨文化交际往往不是各行其是的结果,而是遵循了共同的礼仪准则的成果。因此,本书所介绍的礼仪知识均以"通行"为准绳,而不是分国罗列。

本书不仅有助于读者了解我国与西方国家的礼仪文化差异,对于人们日常交际也有一定的指导作用。其适用于大专院校非英语专业学生的英语国际礼仪课程学习,也可作为希望提高自身英语应用能力及日常交际技巧的社会人士的业余读物,希望此书可以使不同层面的读者朋友受益。

全书的教学可设 54 学时,其中讲授 36 学时,实践 18 学时,不同的使用群体可以根据实际情况增加或减少实践学时。

对于本书的出版,诸多老师和同行都给予了大力的协助。大连外国语学院杨俊峰教授的国际礼仪及文化差异讲座对于此书的创作和编写有极大的启发,在此向杨俊峰教授致以衷心的感谢。编者有幸邀请到东北师范大学原副校长、博士生导师杨忠教授为本书作序,在此向杨忠教授致以诚挚的谢意。北京大学出版社编辑李颖女士对于此书的出版给予了中肯的建议和热心的督促,使本书得以尽早与读者见面。

本书是对国际礼仪知识的一次尝试性的总结和介绍,由于编者水平有限,定会有诸多不足之处,恳望专家学者和广大读者批评指正。

编　者
2009 年 8 月

ACKNOWLEDGEMENTS

The aim of this text book is to introduce international business etiquettes and cross-cultural communication skills to Chinese readers and students. We are indebted to many sources for the passages and pictures selected for reading. With regard to the issue of copyright, we have made extensive efforts to contact the publishers and authors of these passages and pictures, but for various reasons we have been unable to establish communication in some cases. In these cases we apologize to the publishers and authors in advance and will be happy to make fuller acknowledgement in due course. For any questions concerning copyright and permissions, please contact.

Telephone: +86 43185098528
E-mail: zzyouweir@yahoo.cn

We will be happy to make any necessary arrangements for the appropriate settlement of any possible copyright issues.

Contents

Chapter I

Why Etiquette?

Louis XIV's gardener at Versailles was faced with a serious problem: he could not stop members of the nobility from trampling about in the delicate areas of the King's garden. He finally attempted to dissuade their unwanted behavior by posting signs, called etiquets, which warned them to "keep off the grass." When this course of action failed, the King himself had to issue an official decree that no one could go beyond the bounds of the signs. Later, the name "etiquette" was given to a ticket for court functions that included rules regarding where to stand and what to do.

The word "etiquette" has evolved, and in many ways it still means "keep off the grass"—remaining within the flexible boundaries of civil behavior allows relationships and us to grow like flowers in Louis' garden. Moreover, it lets us present ourselves with confidence and authority in all areas of our professional and personal life.

Why is etiquette important in interpersonal communication?

The importance of etiquette is thousands of years old: Around 2500 B.C. the first etiquette manuscript gave this advice to young Egyptian men on the fast track, "When sitting with one's superior, laugh when he laughs (*The Instructions of Ptahhotep*);" and an old Chinese saying goes that you will offend no one by being as courteous as possible.

In our society, good manners are considered an important part of a cultured person's upbringing. Your inability to handle yourself as expected could be expensive. No one will tell you the real reason why you didn't get the job, the promotion, or the social engagement. Fair or not, others equate bad manners with incompetence and a lack of breeding. On the contrary, by being polite, you will not just "offend no one," but you can also please almost everyone.

But why do we more and more easily get confused about good manners or, say, etiquette? How does it happen that sometimes we try to impress others in a polite way but it turns out to be just the opposite of what we wished?

To find out the reasons, first we must know what etiquette is.

In the story at the beginning of this chapter, etiquette means "rules regarding where to stand and what to do" in the court and "remaining within the flexible boundaries of civil behavior," which "allows relationships and us to grow like flowers in Louis' garden."

In most dictionaries, the word "etiquette" is defined as "the formal rules of proper (social) behavior" (Longman, 2005), "the customary code of polite behavior in society or among members of a particular profession or group" (Oxford, 2007), "the set of rules or customs which control accepted behavior in particular social groups or social situations" (Cambridge, 2004), and the like.

American etiquette expert Emily Post defined etiquette as, "Whenever two people come together and their behavior affects one another, you have etiquette. Etiquette is not some rigid code of manners; it's simply how persons' lives touch one another." She believed that etiquette is not about rules, but about building relationships.

Based on Emily Post's definition, her great-granddaughter-in-law Peggy Post explained that "Etiquette gives us clues as to how we should act and what we should do in any given situation, so that we can be as successful as possible in our interactions with the people around us."

According to the common key words in the definitions listed above, we can therefore draw the conclusion that etiquette is about the acceptable standards of human behaviors when there is more than one person in given situations. All is relative. That is to say, etiquette can be different when there are different people and/ or when people are in different situations; and moreover, what is polite to one person can be offensive to another.

In our life, especially in the current situation of globalization, the interacting people probably come from different countries, use different languages, have different social and cultural backgrounds, and therefore certainly have different understandings of etiquette. It is consequently inevitable for us to be occasionally in breach of the etiquette in others' eyes, and it is challenging but essential for us to know about others' understandings of etiquette, find similarities between theirs and our own, bridge the gap of communication caused by the differences in understanding "etiquette," and set standards of behaviors that can be accepted and met by all people regardless of cultural, social, and national differences, so that we can succeed in cross-cultural communication in the global workplace.

Learning international business etiquette suits well our purpose of successful communication.

I. ALL THAT IS ABOUT INTERNATIONAL BUSINESS ETIQUETTE

Every culture has its own time-honored protocols, and the way you first connect with someone from a different culture is critical to establishing a relationship that will be mutually beneficial.

International Business Etiquette refers to the behavior guidance applicable throughout the world for international business persons to establish harmonious relationships in the global working environment and to smooth the way to all business activities.

Though most of its specific rules are originated from European and American social etiquette, international business etiquette is based on the universality of etiquette of different countries all over the world and it embraces the various rules of proper behavior that are the most typical of different cultures. It is agreed upon through long-term cross-cultural blending—in communications and compromises, even in misunderstandings and conflicts.

In this book, everyday business etiquette in activities such as dress and grooming, visiting and receiving, meeting and greeting, dining, and interview is introduced to the readers in great detail.

II. THE CHARACTERISTICS OF INTERNATIONAL BUSINESS ETIQUETTE
EQUALITY AND PRIORITY

For all the individuals in international business activities, they are supposed to be equal in taking the responsibility of observing the same business etiquette, regardless of their age, gender, race and nationality. For example, in traditional western etiquette, if a gentleman and a lady are to shake hands, the gentleman should not extend his hand until the lady does. While shaking the lady's hand, instead of holding her hand tightly, the gentleman should gently hold the front of her hand to pay his tribute. Likewise, if a senior and a junior are to shake hands, the latter should wait until the former extends his hand. However, in international business etiquette, it's advised that both sides extend their hands initiatively. (*For the exceptions, please check Chapter III.*)

On the other hand, in business activities, the individuals' roles vary according to aims of the business actions. In some cases, priority should be given to some people to show respect. For instance, in business receptions, when the guests are getting aboard the cars, the most distinguished guest should be arranged at the right seat of the back. The receptionist should take the seat beside the driver.

● **SPECIALTY AND UNIVERSALITY**

Different countries have different cultures and customs, such as habits, preferences and taboos. This entails the various etiquettes in business receptions and other business actions. These etiquettes are the very core of international business etiquettes. To avoid the cultural barriers, more and more business persons have realized the importance of understanding and respecting the others' cultures and etiquettes. For example, normally, Chinese people use chopsticks, whereas the westerners use fork and knife. However, when a Chinese business person is invited to a dinner party of the western style by his foreign friends, he would use the fork and knife instead of the chopsticks, and vice versa. As the saying goes, "when in Rome, do as the Romans do," people's adaptation to different cultures promotes the cross-cultural communication of business.

However, today's globalization requires the business persons of various backgrounds to understand and observe the universal international business etiquettes in order to fulfill their plan in business activities. A simple example could make this point clear. When the representatives from different countries come to China to have an international conference, they could not communicate with each other in their own languages, nor could they use Chinese. They would routinely use English as the official language. The internationalization and globalization of business activities makes it essential to understand the universality of international business etiquette. For this reason, this book would focus on the details of universal business etiquette while introducing the typical cultural differences of some countries at the same time.

● **CULTURAL AND CROSS–CULTURAL FEATURES**

Although international business etiquette is defined as guidance to the proper behaviors and harmonious communication in international business activities, it is not only the creature of the business activities themselves. International business etiquette is closely related to the humane and natural features, such as the histories of all the countries, their politics, regional characteristics, religions, ethnics and languages. It is greatly possessed of cultural characteristics. Simultaneously, while understanding and observing international business etiquette in the global working environment, the business persons of different cultural backgrounds enhance the development of multicultural communication and accelerate the cross-cultural blending.

III. THE PRINCIPLES THAT GOVERN ALL ETIQUETTES

● RESPECT AND SINCERITY

In interpersonal communication, what an individual does and how he does it will influence not only himself, but also the others who are in touch with him. To respect the others is the essential etiquette in interpersonal communication. Respect is often displayed in the trifles, such as listening to the others attentively, not interrupting the other's conversation, remembering the names of new acquaintances, replying promptly to the letters, phone calls and messages. Of course, being respectful does not mean betraying yourself, or compromising your integrity, which will make others feel that you are phony. Sincerity is the foundation of respect, and it wins you the respect from the others.

● CONSIDERATION AND FLEXIBILITY

Treating the others politely is to make the interpersonal relationship harmonious and to make all the people feel comfortable in communication. So sometimes, to achieve this goal, we have to abandon the doctrines and take humans as essentials. We need to look at the current situation and assess how it affects everyone who is involved in the stereotype of "good manners" but fail to make everyone comfortable. Well-intentioned as it is, this kind of behavior is improper. To bend the rules is also one important part of business etiquette. The story of the hostess and the fingerbowl might be known to you. The fingerbowl is used to wash one's fingers before one eats the food with one's hand. (*For details, please check Chapter V.*) The hostess' guest of honor knew nothing about it and drank the water in the fingerbowl. Before other guests could react, the hostess followed the guest of honor without hesitation. She bent the rule to set the guest of honor free from embarrassment and made herself role model of all hostesses. On the other hand, from the thoughtless behavior of this guest of honor, we learned that when we are not sure about what to do and/or how to do it, wait and follow the others.

● GRATITUDE AND GENEROSITY

While the other people treat you courteously or do you a small favor, don't take it for granted. It should be noticed and remembered that your comfortable situation is made possible by the others' efforts and kindness. Please accept this courtesy with gratitude. In everyday life, please say "please" and "thank you" as much as possible (you will not say "please" and "thank you" for too many times); you might want to return the others' favor by offering a hand when it is in need. Please show your generosity and offer the most courtesy of yours.

After discussing over the definitions, characteristics and principles of international business etiquette, I would like to share with the readers a little humorous story: A French boy moved to Britain with his parents. On his first school-day in a foreign country, when he returned home, his parents asked whether he was happy at school. He answered, obviously upset, "Not at all, because all my classmates spoke English and I could not understand a word of theirs." After a pause, however, the French boy looked a little happier and said, "But they laughed in French." Besides humor, the naivety of the little boy also tells us that verbal language is not the only way of communication. On some occasions, non-verbal means such as facial expressions can be more effective than languages for conveying information. In this sense, international business etiquette is more like the laugh that can be understood and affect others even when different languages cause barriers to communication, as long as we respect others from the bottom of our hearts, always follow the universally acknowledged guidance, and be considerate and flexible enough to know when not to follow it.

To sum up, etiquette is the link between tradition and fashion, and the bridge between culture and culture. Etiquette greases the wheels of interaction in business, in society and in the whole world. Being comfortable in a variety of environments and cultures is one of the end results of etiquette training. People educated and trained with international business etiquette know better about the importance of harmony in work and in life.

Chapter II

Dress the Part, Look the Part

Although the reason for our primitive ancestors' getting dressed could be as simple as that they needed to shelter themselves from natural threats to their lives such as cold and heat, clothing is a sign of the development of human civilization. In the *Holy Bible*, the first proof that Adam and Eve came to know good and evil after eating the fruit to make them wise was that when they opened their eyes and found themselves both naked, they sewed fig leaves together to make themselves aprons. No matter what the reasons are, we human beings spend almost all our waking hours, and even sleeping time, whether when we are alone or with others, dressed; and we naturally hide ourselves from the presence of others without right clothes on us. Clothing is so indispensable to civilized human life that it is like our skin, special skin that can help tell one individual from another, and distinguish human beings from other creatures.

Admittedly it is not advisable to judge people by appearances, but, to a large extent, our dresses and appearances help us make good impressions on others; at the same time, dressing ourselves appropriately shows our respect to the people around. People communicate with one another by dress and grooming, and sometimes in the business world, dress and grooming can be more effective than languages as means of communication.

Section One Business Attire

In our life, styles of clothing vary from occasion to occasion. Social and business occasions roughly fall into three categories: formal, casual and informal, based on which what we wear can also be divided into formal wear, casual wear and informal wear. Since there are almost no informal occasions in the business world, we will discuss over business formal and business casual clothes.

I. FORMAL CLOTHES

Formal clothes are worn on certain formal occasions at work such as interviews, receiving customers, negotiations, reception banquets and anniversary ceremonies. At parties or on daily social occasions including concerts, weddings and funerals, formal clothes are also expected. Formal clothes can be divided into morning attire and evening attire.

1. Morning Attire

Morning attire is worn on most formal occasions in the day. It is so practical that it is suitable for almost all situations and can be worn every day. Black suits, the most formal among morning attire, are worn on solemn occasions such as funerals. Black suits are also called the morning dress.

MORNING ATTIRE FOR MEN

Morning attire for men refers to the outfit of men's suit, shirt, tie, socks, shoes and accessories. The attire will be discussed item by item in the respective categories of fabrics or material, design and color.

Suit

Suit is the formal clothes that can be worn to work every day and is an essential in a businessman's wardrobe, although nowadays business people are dressing themselves more and more casually. While you want to select a suit with care, think less of making a fashion statement than of finding something that fits well and feels comfortable, and that will stand the test of time.

There is only one ironclad rule in choosing a fabric for a suit: No matter what the color is, the surface should be matte—not shiny or iridescent. According to Peggy Post, the choice in fabrics mainly boils down to wool or cotton. With its many textures, wool is undoubtedly the suit fabric of choice because of its ability to stretch yet still keep its shape; its matte finish; its ability to breathe (keeping you warmer in winter and cooler in summer); and its long shelf life. In summer, cotton and linen are popular suit fabrics because they're so comfortable. But be especially careful with linen, because it is very easy to be wrinkled.

Men's suit can be divided into two-piece suit and three-piece suit. A two-piece suit refers to the outfit of the jacket and the pants, and a three-piece suit refers to the outfit of the jacket, the vest and the pants. Three-piece suits are more traditional and formal than two-piece ones. There are usually few buttons (single or double lines, two or three buttons per line) and one or two slits (along the middle line if one, along the two sides if two) on the open-necked jacket of the suit.

Dark colors have always been associated with authority, but tradition has also embraced suits in lighter shades of brown (tan and beige) and grey. Solids are always a safe choice, while pinstripes are a handsome alternative, with a very thin, light grey stripe preferred. Black suits are too solemn for daily occasions. Suits with check patterns on them are not viewed as formal wear.

Dress Shirt

Non-sleeveless white cotton or woolen shirts are the dressiest choice at work. White shirts with white collars are the most popular attire for business people. This is probably why business men and women are called "the white collar".

Dress shirts have square collars, short collars or long collars. The sleeves of the dress shirt should be a bit longer than those of the jacket and the collar of the dress shirt should be a bit higher than that of the jacket.

More muted colors, preferably solid, work better than loud ones. Besides white shirts, blue, grey and dark brown ones are acceptable, too. The only caveat is to make sure that the jacket, the shirt and the tie complement one another. Pinstripe has already become the practical and popular pattern of dress shirts. But keep in mind that the color of the stripes and the base color of the shirt should not conflict each other; at the same time, be careful to coordinate pinstriped suits, because sometimes such coordination could be "noisy" to others' eyes. Check-patterned shirts are not acceptable on formal occasions.

Tie/Necktie

For the great majority of men who dress for business, the tie remains the most important of all accessories.

Ties are mainly made of silk fabrics. And the standard length of a necktie is 140 cm, allowing a margin of 10 cm longer or shorter than that. The widest part of the wide end is about 7—10 cm. The point of the wide end of a traditional necktie is the point of a right-angular arrow.

Regardless of the design, make sure your tie color coordinates with your shirt and jacket. Solid-colored neckties without patterns are the dressiest choice of formal coordination, and ties with geometrical patterns such as pinstripes, small spots and small checks are acceptable too. Do not wear a tie with more than three colors, or with loud patterns or cartoon patterns.

When the tying of the necktie is done, the point of the wide end should be right over the upper edge of the buckle of the belt. Then secure the tie with a tie clip. Coordinated with a three-piece suit, the lower part of the tie should be secured between the shirt and the vest, not between the vest and the jacket.

Shoes

Always wear smooth-surface leather shoes!

Rough-surface leather shoes or suede shoes can not be coordinated with formal suits.

Colors of the shoes should be coordinated to or darker than those of the suits. Among the choices, black ranks No. 1, with dark brown second to it.

Socks

Socks are mostly made from cotton or silk.

With the proper length of your socks, you will avoid exposing the skin of your legs to others while seated.

Colors of the socks are always dark and solid, preferably black, coordinated to the shoes.

The most common and embarrassing faux pas of Chinese business persons wearing western suits is that most of them wear white socks together with black shoes. The contrast is so obvious that it can hardly be neglected.

Accessories

Men wear LEATHER BELTS or SUSPENDERS coordinated respectively with their shoes and to their ties. The width of the belts is about 3 cm and the buckles can be either metal or leather. If metal, the buckle should be coordinated to other metal accessories such as the tie pin and the watchband. The alternative (attention: NOT a companion) to a belt is suspenders, which are not about function, but style. The quietness or wildness of the pattern of suspenders depends on the company culture in which the wearer operates.

The function of a TIE CLIP/TIE PIN is to secure the tie. Therefore, the wearer should wear it at a place so that it can be hidden from the spot of others, for example, the interval between the fourth and the fifth button of the shirt (from top to bottom). There can be only one accessory, namely only ONE tie clip, for the necktie.

The JEWELRY that men can wear with morning suits is limited to watches and rings. The maximum of rings worn by a businessman is one per hand, preferably just one—the wedding or engagement band.

Laptop computer cases are now challenging the traditional rectangular black leather BRIEFCASE in popularity. Whichever you use, it should be in excellent condition. For a simple sheaf of papers, another option is a leather envelope carried under the arm.

MORNING ATTIRE FOR WOMEN

Morning attire for women refers to the outfit consisting of suit, blouse, scarf, stocking/knee-highs, shoes and accessories. Like men's, the attire will be discussed item by item in the respective categories of fabrics or material, design and color.

Suit

Fabrics of women's suits are the same as those of men's suits (See Page 8).

There are both two-piece and three-piece suits for women. A two-piece suit refers to the outfit of jacket and pants or the outfit of jacket and skirt. A three-piece suit refers to the outfit of jacket, pants and skirt, but pants and skirt are certainly not to be worn together. A skirt suit is more traditional and formal than a pant suit. The jacket is usually open-necked, with a few buttons (single or double lines, one or two buttons per line) and no slit at the back (not like men's). The minimal length of the jacket is that its bottom rim reaches the waist. The ideal length of the skirt is that it reaches about 2.5 cm above or below the knees. The longest skirt will reach the plumpest part of the shins. Traditional skirts have slits at the back, along the middle line. Nowadays there are more and more original designs and beautiful ornaments adding to women's suit, relieving the rigidity while keeping the elegancy.

Wearing suits, women have more choices of colors than men do. In addition to the traditional dark colors such as navy blue, burgundy, taupe and charcoal grey, neutral colors such as sea green, camel and peach are also acceptable. In a word, many colors can be worn as long as bright orange, magenta, and other loud and flashy colors are avoided. All in all, when in doubt, tone the colors down with a dark color. Solid-colored suits without patterns are safe. Stripes, checks, small spots and other geometrical patterns, however, add energy to the outfit. Anyway, avoid loud patterns and cartoon patterns.

Blouse

Women wear non-sleeveless blouses inside their suits. Fabrics of blouses are mostly cotton. Solid light colors such as white, cream, ivory, eggshell and pearl are acceptable, among which white and cream are the safest as far as coordination to the suit is concerned.

Scarf

Silk, yarn, cashmere or cotton scarves (Silk is the best choice.) can heighten focus on the face or provide visual relief in a monochromatic outfit. Scarves can also dress up a casual outfit or soften a tailored look. Coordinate a multicolored scarf to your ensemble by making sure it picks up a color in the outfit.

Stockings and Knee-Highs

Flexible skin-color silk stockings and knee-highs are worn to match women's skirt suits. Only clean stockings or knee-highs can be worn with suits, and there should be no runs on them. The rims of stockings or knee-highs should not be exposed to others. Stockings or knee-highs like net or with large patterns are not acceptable at workplace or on formal occasions.

Pumps

Shoes that match the morning suit should be dark-color, smooth-surface leather ones. As for color, black is the safest choice, and other quiet and conservative colors are also acceptable as long as they go well with the suit. Women's shoes should cover all their toes and heels of feet. And the height of the shoe heels—in good condition, not worn down ones—ranges from 2.5 to 4 cm.

Accessories

When a woman's outfit requires a BELT, the classic style is a leather one whose width ranges from approximately 1.3 cm to 2 cm. The buckle can be metal or leather in any simple, quiet shape. If the buckle is metal, it should be coordinated to other metal—earrings, necklaces, watchbands, buttons. The belt's color should harmonize with shoe and garment colors.

The JEWELRY that a woman can choose to match her morning attire includes earrings, necklaces, bracelet, wristwatch and rings, which are made of gold, silver, platinum or pearls. The watchband can be made of stainless steel or leather. Keep in mind that at traditional offices, you should let nothing dangle, jangle, sparkle or be gaudy. With simplicity as the guiding principle, limit the amount of jewelry you wear to 4 pieces. The maximum number of rings for traditional business wear is one per hand (wedding and engagement band count as one ring).

In terms of HANDBAG, Peggy Post says, "a quality handbag is a valuable accessory". Focus first on neatness and functionality, making sure the bag is large enough to hold all the items you carry with you other than makeup—a day planner, for example.

DOS AND DON'TS OF WEARING MORNING ATTIRE

- Avoid wearing the clothes that are not of your size. Preferably have your beautifully tailored ones in your wardrobe.
- Before wearing the suit, do remember to tear off the trade mark label (usually on the sleeves).
- Do have your suits, your shirts and your ties ironed before you wear them. Do not wear wrinkled clothes.
- For gentlemen: Do fasten all the buttons on the suit jacket, or fasten all but the last one at the bottom; do not keep the coat all unbuttoned or only fasten the last button at the bottom; do fasten all buttons on the shirt (including the sleeve buttons or cuff links).
- For ladies: Do fasten all the buttons on the suit jacket; do never keep the coat unbuttoned; do fasten all the buttons on the blouse (sometimes the first button at the top can be left unfastened); do never take off the suit jacket with people surrounding you.
- Before getting dressed, do examine your clothes to see whether they are in good condition, because sometimes it just happens that one of the buttons has come off your shirt or there are runs on your stockings.
- Women should wear belts loose enough to ride with the waistband of your skirt/ pants, not above it.
- Do not forget to correctly fasten your buttons and do remember to do up your flies.
- Do not roll up the sleeves of your shirt/blouse or your suit.
- Do never, ever, roll up your trouser legs.
- Generally speaking, V-neck sweaters are not acceptable on formal occasions, although it is not unusual that V-neck sweaters are worn between suits and shirts by gentlemen. If the weather is cold, a three-piece suit is a better choice than a two-piece one and a solid dark-color overcoat is preferably worn over the suit, which can be taken off as soon as the wearer enters a room with

central heating or air-conditioning.

- Do not wear smelly shoes or socks. Keep your socks clean and have your shoes polished.
- Do not wear too many colors. Try to limit them to three.
- On formal occasions, whether you are men or women, do dress yourself professional, not too sexy or too trendy.
- If you are not sure that you dress yourself appropriately for certain situations, do err on the conservative side.
- Some office ladies lay such great emphasis on the equality between men and women that they refuse to wear skirt suits, because they believe there should be no difference between the clothes of business MEN and business WOMEN and pant suits make them look as professional as men. In fact, however, if you are confident and competent enough, you will forget the difference of genders in the business world, which means equality in a real sense. Choose the clothes that fit YOU well (not fit men well, or fit women well), you will look professional whether in pant suits or in skirt suits.

Wow! There are so many details of getting ourselves formally dressed. How can we remember the full details and be sure to dress up appropriately? Don't worry! The tables on page 33 and page 34 can brief you on wearing morning attire in an easy and quick way.

2. Evening Attire

As the term suggests, evening attire is worn in the evening, usually after 6:00 p.m., on such occasions as banquets, opening ceremonies and concerts.

EVENING SUIT (for men)

Tails

Tails with white bow tie and black leather shoes are worn for the ultimate formal event. Usually this type of dress would be required for a fundraiser such as the Academy Ball in Philadelphia, the Presidential Inaugural Ball in Washington DC, the first performance in the opera house, the grand opening ceremony and various charity events. Very formal weddings also use this attire to differentiate the wedding party from the guests who are attending dressed in tuxedos.

Tuxedo/Dinner Jacket

Tuxedo is also called dinner jacket. It's usually worn for formal or semiformal occasions. Tuxedo jackets often include satin on the lapels that are attached to the collars. Tuxedo pants resemble men's tailored trousers except that they generally have a satin or ribbon stripe sewn over the outside seam of the leg. Most tuxedos are worn with specific accessories that include the slightly stiffened, sometimes fancy, white pleated shirt that closes with old-fashioned shirt studs rather than buttons. Another important accessory is the cummerbund or fabric belt that encircles the waistband of the trousers and secures in the back. Tuxedo may be sewn from a wide variety of colors and fabrics; increasingly, brighter colors and unconventional designs are pervasive in tuxedo styling. Nevertheless, most tuxedos are produced in black.

Bow Tie

The bow tie is a men's necktie popularly worn with formal attire, such as suits or dinner jackets. It consists of a ribbon of fabric tied around the collar in a symmetrical manner such that the two opposite ends form loops. Bow ties may be made of silk, polyester, cotton, or a mixture of fabrics. Colors of bow ties are generally white and black. White bow ties match tails and black bow ties match tuxedoes.

EVENING DRESS (for women)

Lady's evening dress is also called evening gown or banquet dress, a long, flowing lady's dress that is usually worn to a formal affair. It ranges in length from ballerina to full-length. Gowns are often made of a luxury fabric such as chiffon, velvet, satin, or silk. As for the accessories, a pashmina shawl, silk cashmere stole, a matching necklace, earrings and bracelets will highlight the rest of the ensemble.

CHINESE TUNIC SUIT, CHEONGSAM AND TANG SUIT

Tunic suit

Tunic suit was originally designed with the supervision of Dr. Sun Yat-sen and then named after this great pioneer of Chinese democratic revolution. It's simple in design, shaped to the body and elegant in style. In China, it's dressed in formal situations, such as the national celebrations, the state banquets and the decorations. It's accepted internationally as one of Chinese formal dresses.

Cheongsam

The western evening dress for ladies is often designed for the plump figure of westerners. The low-necked expansion skirt highlights the breast and back. Compared with the western evening dress, Chinese **cheongsam** suits Chinese ladies better. The cheongsam is a female dress with distinctive Chinese features and enjoys a growing popularity in the international world of high fashion. It's neatly tailored, easy to slip on and comfortable to wear and fits well the female Chinese figure. Its neck is high, collar closed, and its sleeves may be short, medium or full length, depending on season and taste. The dress is buttoned on the right side, with a loose chest, a fitting waist, and slits up from the sides, all of which combine to set off the beauty of the female shape. It's usually made of brocade or silk. It's suitable for many social events, formal or casual, and the simple and quiet charm it displays attracts the women not only of China but of foreign countries as well.

Tang Suit

With the international popularity of Chinese taste, Tang suit has been accepted by the people all over the world. Tang suit carries the festive merry feeling and sociability. In Chinese festivities and celebrations such as Spring Festival evening party, Tang suit is dressed by both Chinese and foreign guests to express their happiness and wishes for the coming new year.

II. CASUAL CLOTHES

Casual clothes are also called semi-formal clothes and are more and more commonly worn by business people in their daily working environment. They are not as rigid as formal clothes and people usually feel more relaxed and comfortable and even closer to one another in casual clothes than they do in formal ones. Many companies have "casual Friday" policy, which allows, even encourages employees to wear casual clothes at work on Friday or any other day of the week. When wearing causal clothes, business people have more choices of their clothes' fabrics, colors and patterns than they do when wearing formal ones. Please remember that the word "casual" describes more the styles of the clothes than your attitude toward work and business, and that you may also probably meet your customers and receive your guests although you are casually dressed; so, always be prepared and do not be too "casual." Besides, it is advisable not to wear casual clothes for such formal occasions as interviews, negotiations and business receptions. Examples of acceptable casual clothes for men are: blazers or sport jackets, oxford-style shirts with button-down collars, turtleneck shirts, short sleeved knit shirts, khaki slacks, v-neck or crew-neck sweaters and informal ties. Examples of acceptable casual clothes for women are: casual blazers over nice-quality plain knit blouses, tailored pants or Bermuda-length shorts (depend on locale), jumper-style dress (long or short), khaki pants, washable linen pants, twin sweater sets, tunic-style sweaters, loafers or flats and open-toed pumps. The following picture illustrates business causal clothes for men and women.

Illustration Samples

Business Casual for Women

Business Casual for Men

Section Two   Tying Ties and Scarves

In this section, basic ways of tying ties will be introduced especially to gentlemen and basic ways of tying scarves will be introduced to ladies.

I. TYING TIES

It is universally accepted that gentlemen are not as skillful as and less interested than ladies in all the tying stuff. As a gentleman, however, one should know at least one way of tying a tie. And I sincerely recommend that gentlemen not wear a convenient necktie on business occasions.

1. Windsor Knot

The Windsor knot is a thick, wide and triangular tie knot that projects confidence. It would therefore be your knot of choice for presentations, job interviews, courtroom appearances etc. It is best suited for spread collar shirts and it's actually quite easy to do.

While just about everyone can use this tie knot to tie his tie, it looks especially well on men with longer necks as its wide form shortens the perceived height of the neck a little bit.

To tie the Windsor knot, select a tie of your choice and stand in front of a mirror. Then simply follow the steps below:

1) The wide end "W" should extend about 30.5cm below narrow end "N." Cross wide end "W" over narrow end "N."

2) Bring wide end "W" up through loop between collar and tie; then back down.

3) Pull wide end "W" underneath narrow end "N" and to the left, back through the loop and to the left again so that the wide end "W" is inside out.

4) Bring wide end "W" across the front from left to right.

5) Pull wide end "W" up through the loop again.

6) Bring wide end "W" down through the knot in front.

7) Using both hands, tighten the knot carefully and draw up to collar.

2. Half Windsor Knot

The Half Windsor Knot, a modest version of the Windsor knot, is a symmetrical and triangular tie knot that you can use with any dress shirt. It works best with somewhat wider ties made from light to medium fabrics.

To tie the Half Windsor Knot, select a tie of your choice and stand in front of a mirror. Then simply follow the steps below:

1) The wide end "W" should extend about 30.5cm below narrow end "N." Cross wide end "W" over narrow end "N."

2) Bring wide end "W" up around and behind narrow end "N."

3) Bring wide end "W" up.

4) Pull wide end "W" up and through the loop.

5) Bring wide end "W" around front, over narrow end "N" from left to right.

6) Again, bring wide end "W" up and through the loop.

7) Bring wide end "W" down through the knot in front.

8) Using both hands, tighten the knot carefully and draw up to collar.

3. Four-in-Hand Knot

Also known as a simple knot, the four-in-hand is believed to be the most popular method of tying ties due to its simplicity. The knot produced by this method is on the narrow side, slightly asymmetric, and appropriate for all occasions. It works best with wide ties made from heavy fabrics and should be worn with a tab, button-down or regular spread collar. It's a classic and most widely used knot.

To tie the four-in-hand knot, select a tie of your choice and stand in front of a mirror. Then simply follow the steps below:

1) The wide end "W" should extend about 30.5cm below narrow end "N." Cross wide end "W" over narrow end "N."

2) Turn wide end "W" back underneath narrow end "N."

3) Continue by bringing wide end "W" back over in front of narrow end "N" again.

4) Pull wide end "W" up and through the loop around your neck.

5) Hold the front of the knot loosely with your index finger and bring wide end "W" down through front loop.

6) Remove finger and tighten knot carefully to collar by holding narrow end "N" and sliding the knot up.

4. Bow Tie Knot

The Bow Tie Knot is used to tie a bow tie and is worn to give you a formal and elegant appearance.

The proper size should never be broader than the widest part of your neck and should never extend past the tips of the shirt collar.

Ready-tied bow ties are available, in which the distinctive bow is sewn into shape and the band around the neck incorporates a clip. Some "clip-ons" dispense with the band altogether, instead of clipping to the collar. The traditional bow tie, consisting of a strip of cloth which the wearer has to tie by hand, may be known as a "self-tie," "tie-to-tie," or "freestyle" bow tie to distinguish it from these.

To tie the Bow Tie Knot, select a bow tie of your choice and stand in front of a mirror. Then simply follow the steps below:

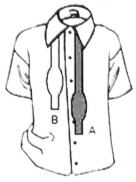

1) Place the bow tie around your neck, situating it so that end "A" is about 5.1cm longer than end "B."

2) Cross end "A" over end "B."

3) Bring end "A" up and under the loop.

4) Now double end "B" over itself to form the front base loop of the bow tie.

5) Loop end "A" over the center of the loop you just formed.

6) Holding everything in place, double end "A" back on itself and poke it through the loop behind the bow tie.

7) Adjust the bow tie by tugging at the ends of it and straightening the center knot.

II. TYING SCARVES

An elaborately chosen and delicately tied scarf which matches the business suit can enhance both a lady's professionalism and her glamour. Therefore, a smart office lady ensures that there are always at least two scarves in her top drawer and that she is skillful in tying a scarf in at least two ways.

1. Basic Ways to Fold a Scarf

There are three basic ways to fold a scarf:

Triangle

Lay the scarf out flat, and bring two opposite corners together.

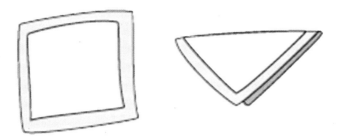

Oblong

Lay the scarf out flat, then fold two opposite sides inwards, one after the other. Repeat until the scarf is your required width.

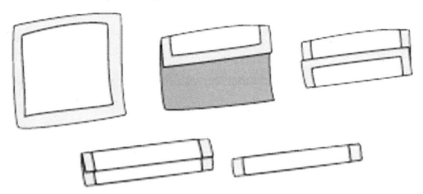

On the Bias

a. Lay the scarf out flat, then take two opposite corners and fold them into the centre, one after the other. Repeat until the scarf is your required width.

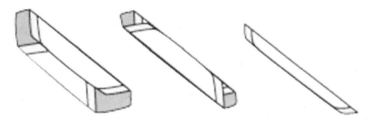

b. For a fuller look, first fold the scarf into a triangle then, starting at the point, carefully roll the scarf up into a long thin strip.

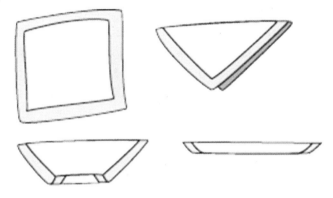

2. Knots of Bandanas

A Bandana refers to a small square scarf whose size is 45cmx45cm as a standard.

Butterfly Knot

This knot can be worn with almost any top. To tie the butterfly knot, select a scarf of your choice and stand in front of a mirror. Then simply follow the steps below:

1) Fold a bandana in a strip.

2) Tie a loose knot like a ring at one end.

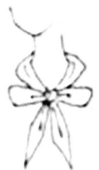
3) Wrap the bandana round your neck. Pull the other end through the ring. Adjust the knot like butterfly.

Done!

Square Knot

This knot is best worn with an open neckline or a collared dress shirt. This makes a smooth, well proportioned knot that lies flat. It is really a double knot—take care to do the actual tying with the same end of the scarf for both knots. To tie the square knot, select a scarf of your choice and stand in front of a mirror. Then simply follow the steps below:

1) Fold along the bias and put the strip around your neck.

2) Grasp the two ends and drape behind around neck so that one end hangs lower than the other. Cross long end over the short end. Bring it up through the loop created.

3) Take the same end and wrap around behind short end. Pull long end across and insert horizontally through the knot created, forming a square.

4) Adjust the knot as shown

Done!

3. Knots of Long Scarves

A long scarf usually refers to either a 45cm×150cm oblong scarf or a 90cm×90cm square one. As for the following two knots, the former fits a 90cm×90cm while the latter fits a 45cm×150cm.

Goldfish Knot

This knot works best when filling a bare neckline. To tie the goldfish knot, select a scarf of your choice and stand in front of a mirror. Then simply follow the steps below:

1) Fold a scarf in strip folds. Hang the scarf around your neck. Make two ends across each other, placing the shorter end on top.

2) Pull the shorter end through loop and make a loose knot. Take the longer end back to the knot and make a ring.

3) Pull the back end around the ring and then from the top go through the knot.

4) Tighten the knot and adjust until it looks like a gold fish

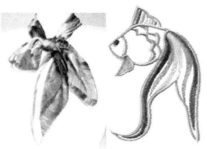

Alike?

Twisting Knot

This knot works best when filling a bare neckline.

1) Hold a long scarf in halfway folds. Twist it and hang around your neck. Only allow End A to pass through the loop.

2) Hold A and B and twist both until they reach your collar.

3) Take A and B through the loop as directed.

4) Adjust both ends.

Done!

Section Three Grooming

In her book *The Etiquette Advantage in Business*, Peggy Post gives a thorough introduction to the secret of appropriate business grooming. The following contents are an excerpt from her work:

Grooming is every bit as important as what you wear, from tip to toe. For example, hair has proved its potential to make a statement as well as or more strongly than clothes do, and the amount of makeup sends an unavoidable message, too—and in most workplaces, understatement in both is key.

I. HYGIENE

Watching your hygiene means staying clean, odor-free and untousled. The better groomed people are, the more points they score in business. The idea is to attract, not repel. Here's an everyday grooming checklist:

1. Hair

Wash your hair often enough to keep it from looking greasy.

A woman will attract attention with her hair when she has a flattering cut or healthy, shiny hair that simply begs to be admired. There's no longer a true rule about the length of women's hair, but on the job, hair should be kept out of the eyes: Tuck it behind your ears, pull it back in a ponytail, or pull it out of your eyes with a barrette. Unusual ornaments or colors (like dyed pink or yellow) are risky. Your hair can be curly, wavy or straight, and the clamps that create an instant upswept twist are also popular and make for a nice professional look.

It is not advisable for men to keep long hair. Men's hair should not cover their ears or foreheads. One morning a week at least, gentlemen should check to see if their nose hairs need to be clipped. Men should also keep an electric shaver at hand to smarten them up.

2. Fingernails

Nails should always be kept clean and trimmed. Dirt mysteriously lurking under the fingernails can be a nightmare. Keep a nail clipper with a cleaning tool in your desk drawer. While trimming the fingernails, push back the cuticles occasionally, too.

The best length for men's nails is with about 1.5mm of white showing.

The best length for women's nails in most business environments is just over the tip of the finger. Clear nail polish is the best choice.

3. Tooth Breath and Body Odor

To keep your breath fresh, you should brush your teeth in the morning, at night and after each meal. Bring your toothbrush to work and brush after lunch. A breath mint or two during the day should keep you from offending.

A daily shower is the best defense against body odor.

II. MAKEUP, PERFUME AND COLOGNE

1. Makeup

Men do not wear makeup. Women, as a rule, use a light touch—makeup should enhance, not dominate.

2. Perfume and Cologne

Like it or not, the perfume a woman wears to the office may be offending someone's nose. For example, if you wear too much perfume to a dinner, the smell will probably ruin others' faculties of smell and taste and therefore spoil their appetites. At the same time, there has been an appreciable jump in the number of people who claim they are "allergic" to most smells in general, especially manufactured ones. If you wear perfume to work, make sure the scent is light and clean, and use the perfume sparingly: if your scent still lingers in the room when you leave someone's office, you're wearing too much. Of course, you can also choose to go to work scent-free.

As for a man, no element of the businessman's wardrobe requires more subtlety than cologne. Wearing too much cologne is even worse at an interview, where the "moderation in all things" approach is the key. The toilet waters that refresh the skin after a shower are probably the best choice for the workday, with full-fledged cologne saved for night.

Section Four Non-Verbal Communication Etiquette

According to a study by a professor at UCLA, besides making your wardrobe fit and be appropriate for the setting, you should also pay attention to your body language, and not forget to smile. 55% percent of the message you communicate is conveyed through your visual appearance, including dress, grooming and non-verbal communicating means such as facial expressions, gestures and postures.

I. BODY LANGUAGE SIGNS

Positive body languages, such as regular eye contact, sitting straight, smiling often and walking with grace and ease, help you win your first impression, while negative ones can probably make the communication turn out a disaster. Here are some common signs of both positive and negative body languages.

- Arms crossed=Defensive
- Brisk erect walk=Confidence
- Foot kicking=Boredom
- Tapping fingers=Impatient
- Hands in pocket=Dejection
- Playing with hair=Lack of confidence
- Biting the nails= Nervousness, Insecurity
- Shuffling feet while seated=Anxious to leave the situation
- Standing with hands on hips=Aggression, Ready to take charge
- Looking down with face turned away=Disbelief
- One finger point: in many countries, pointing with the index finger is considered impolite. The open hand is used instead.

Note that the meanings that these body languages convey may vary from country to country.

II. IMPACT OF PERSONAL SPACE

When two people communicate, between them there is a distance comfortable for the both. The following are the comfortable spaces for different occasions.

- Intimate zone: 15.2—45.6cm
- Personal zone: 45.6cm—1.37m
- Social zone: 1.3m—3.9m
- Public zone: over 4m

Usually when two business people communicate, they will stand about 0.9m apart. Any closer one could invade the other's personal space. Any further you'd be yelling. This distance will vary depending on the country; it is advisable to know the cultural differences before conducting business in a foreign country.

Exercise

Discussion

1. Who are best-dressed celebrities in your eyes? What's his/her dressing style? What can you learn from his/her dressing style?

2. If you have applied for a job and finally come to the interview loop, how would you dress yourself for this interview?

3. We all want to be well dressed, but sometimes we can not afford the delicate dresses. What should we do if we have no proper dresses for some important situations?

4. Your close friend is getting married, as the best man/ maid of honor, how to dress yourself for the wedding?

5. How many ways have you learned to tie ties and scarves? Do you have other ways to make your ties and scarves look better? (Remember, practice makes perfect.)

6. Do you have preferences for the color of business dresses? What should we pay attention to when we put two or more colors together for our clothes?

7. Have you found any examples of inappropriate dressing in our daily life? What are the problems and how to solve them?

8. What are the differences between dresses of western style and Chinese traditional dresses? Which style do you prefer?

9. As a college student, how do you think you can dress yourself appropriately for classes, lectures and other activities on campus? Please give examples.

Men's Morning Attire

Items	Design	Color	Material
Suit	tailored and traditionally designed, 3-piece or 2-piece suit with two or three buttons on the coat	always dark, such as black, dark grey, navy blue	wool, linen
Shirt	dress shirts or oxford button-downs, non-sleeveless	light color, white is the safest choice	cotton, linen
Tie	stripes and usually thin stripes, avoid large or exaggerating patterns such as flowers, animals and cartoon characters	match that of the suit, not the shirt	wool, silk
Shoes	Oxfords, wing tips, or loafers	match that of the suit, sometimes darker than the suit, but never lighter	leather
Socks	long enough so that your skin of shin will not be exposed to others when you sit down	match the color of the shoes, always dark, especially black	cotton
Accessories	minimalism and subtlety (no more than 3 pieces). A wedding band, a good watch, a class ring and cuff links.		

Women's Morning Attire

Items	Design	Color	Material
Suit	tailored and traditionally designed skirt-suit with the length of the skirt about 2.5cm above or below the knees, not too long, not too short. or pant suit, 2-piece or 3-piece suit with two or three buttons on the coat	usually dark, but more choices than men's, burgundy	wool, linen
Blouse	non-sleeveless	solid, white (the safest choice), eggshell, cream, or other conservative colors	cotton, linen
Scarf	traditional, in good condition, standard size—90cm, no loud patterns	match the suit, conservative, not too loud colors	silk
Shoes	pumps, loafer-style shoes or flats, cover ladies' toes and heels, with the heels of the shoes from 2.5cm to 5cm high, no higher than 5cm	goes with the suit, sometimes darker, but never lighter	leather
Stockings	tights (panty hose), knee socks, better no pattern, definitely no runs (ladders)	skin color	silk
Accessories	leather handbag, necklace, earrings, rings, watch, bracelet, etc., but no more than 4 pieces		

Chapter III

Meeting and Greeting

Face-to-face interaction is the most direct interpersonal communication. We make impressions on and have impressions of others more through face-to-face communications than relatively indirect communications such as making phone calls and sending emails. Will complete strangers succeed in communicating? Will they keep further contact with one another after meeting for the first time? Will people build harmonious relationship and profound friendship after several meetings and direct contacts? Whether the answers to these questions are affirmative or negative depend on how people behave when they meet and greet one another.

Professor Yang Junfeng gives a concise and comprehensive summary of the smart ways of introducing people in his serial lectures of international business etiquette. The following three aspects of rules are basically a citation from his generalization.

Section One The Art of Introducing People

I. MAKING PROPER INTRODUCTIONS

1. Basic Rules

It is very logical. You properly introduce a lesser to a more important or senior person. You would introduce:

- a younger person to an older person;
- a gentleman to a lady;
- a guest to a host;
- a junior executive to a senior executive;
- an unofficial person to an official person;
- a peer in your company to a peer in another company;
- a fellow in your own country to a peer from another country;
- a fellow executive to a customer or client.

In a word, when you are introducing people, the person who you address first is the more important or the senior one. See the sample below:

"Mr. Cogwell, I want my daughter, Cynthia, to meet you. Cynthia, this is Mr. Cogwell, president of this company."

Here the speaker introduced his/her daughter to the president of the company. Mr. Cogwell was senior to Cynthia both in rank and in status, even in age, so he was addressed first.

Of course, this introduction broke the rule that we should introduce a man to a woman. We should note that, in business world, when we introduce people, if the basic rules conflict with each other, ranks and status (e.g. unofficial to official, and employee to employer) outweigh ages and genders (e.g. young to old, and man to woman).

When you are introducing a junior person to a senior one, touch the arm of the senior person and say his name first, then, symbolically, in your mind, bring up the junior person to the senior one whose arm you are touching. This is the way you'll remember how to introduce people to people of different ranks and status.

2. Remember to Use Titles When Introducing People

People want to know to whom they're speaking, so that they can make appropriate comments. For example, your brother may be your brother, but when you are introducing him, if he is a judge, he should be referred to as "my brother, Judge William Taylor".

Other cases can be dealt with in the same manner: Refer to "Jennifer Garrett", a woman you know well, as "Dr. Jennifer Garrett"; and introduce "Steve Li", who used to be your college roommate but is of high political or appointive office, as "Steve Li, Project Manager of the World Bank" instead of just "Steve Li", because the people to whom you're presenting him would like to know all that about him.

Frequently Used Titles Are Listed Below:

Mr., Mrs., Miss, Ms. (common);

Doctor, Professor, Judge, President (occupational, academic or corporate);

Sister, Father (religious);

Lady, Lord (royal);

and President, Premier, Judge, Mayor, Governor, General (political or military).

3. Explain Who the People Are When You Introduce Them

When you introduce someone, you should give basic information about who they are. Don't just introduce people by name at a business party without giving their firms or profession or some piece of information that can serve as a jumping off point for conversation in that group.

You can introduce the General Manager of your company as

"This is Mr. John Williams, General Manager of our company. He has been

loyally serving the company for more than 20 years and made great contributions
to its development and success."

4. Say Names Slowly, Clearly and Distinctly

This is for the convenience of the people being introduced to remember each other's name. This can also help avoid the probable embarrassment that they have to ask for the other's name again because they didn't catch it during the unclear introduction.

5. Forgetting Names and Mis-Introductions

If You Forget Someone's Entire Name When You Know Him Well

If you have a total lapse of memory or you mis-introduced someone, don't worry, it happens to us all. Confess on the spot. You will be forgiven, because every single person in this world forgets names. After the apology, reintroduce them, with the forgotten name informed and confirmed, of course. At the awkward moment, quick-witted and humorous remarks can always help you out and relieve the embarrassment.

If Someone Repeatedly Mis-Introduces You

Don't make a dramatic episode out of it, put a big smile on your face and whisper in the person's ear: "Just <u>thought you'd like to</u> know that my name is Jane Merson, not Mason." (The underlined words show politeness.)

Be a Sport

Since it's possible that the person you know has forgotten your name and cannot introduce you, help him out. Stick your hand out and give him your name: "Hello, Jim Schubert, good to see you," to which he will reply: "Jim, did you think I had forgotten your name?" Of course, he has, but everyone is smiling; everyone is happy. Being introduced all around, you have saved the day by simply coming out with your name timely.

II. SELF-INTRODUCTION

On many social and business occasions, when you have the opportunity of introducing yourself to a stranger, you can say, "Hello, I don't think we have met before, I am XXX, a college junior at ABC University, and you are?" Usually the person to whom you are introducing yourself will happily give you his/her information in return so that you can communicate with each other smoothly.

When saying our names, we also need to slow down and pronounce our names slowly, clearly and distinctly. We may feel as though we are exaggerating our names, but it eases the problem of communication. Besides, we can give further details of our names, by saying "my name is Cathy White, Cathy with 'C' (there is also a Kathy with 'K')" and the like.

III. REMEMBERING NAMES

A name means everything to the person you are properly introducing in your business life. It also means everything to the person who you are introducing the newcomer to, who will want to learn the other person's name correctly so that he/she won't be embarrassed later by having to ask for it again. If their names are remembered immediately after the acquaintance, people are flattered. Their egos are enhanced, and relationships become more cordial as a result.

Therefore, we should purposefully remember people's names. The ability to remember names is an outstanding asset and it takes practices. Concentration is the key, and you can also try paying attention to people's last names or associate names with people's physical characteristics.

Section Two   Handshakes

People all over the world greet one another differently: Some bow, some hug, some kiss on each other's cheek, others hold the hands... Among all the ways of greeting, handshake is the most practical and universal. In business situations, an introduction is usually accompanied by a handshake, which is your first physical contact with someone else, flesh to flesh.

I. SHAKE HANDS PROPERLY

1. Posture

Here are the steps that you can follow to shake hands properly: Stand about 1.2 meters away from the other person (If farther, step forward; if nearer, step sideward, not backward, because stepping backward when shaking hands will make the other feel that you are reluctant to do so.); extend your right hand so that your forearm and your upper arm form an approximately 3/4 straight angle; keep the thumb up and the four fingers straightly extended together; touch palms before wrapping the fingers around the other person's hand; shake no more than three times (usually three times) and then separate; shake from your elbow, not your shoulder; while shaking, lean forward a bit, and look into each other's eyes, with a smile on the face, saying such words of greeting as "Nice to meet you" and "How do you do?"

2. A Desirable Handshake

A desirable handshake feels: firm, strong, representative of a person who makes decisions, takes risks, and above all, takes charge; warm and enthusiastic as if you are really glad to meet someone; dry and pleasant to the touch.

3. An Undesirable Handshake

An undesirable handshake feels: hesitant, apologetic, almost as if you were saying "I don't really want to shake your hand, nor am I a decision maker"; wet and clammy, or cold, as though you have been holding an iced drink all day; weak, slippery, lifeless, like a handful of dead fish. Just as negative is the bone crusher handshake, which makes the other person feel in need of having his hand checked.

4. Situations in Which Handshakes Are Needed

When you run into someone you know, when you say goodbye to the same person, when someone comes in from the outside to see you in your office and when he leaves, when someone enters your home or when you enter someone else's home, when you meet someone you know in a restaurant, when you're introduced to people in any business or social situation and when you take leave of them, when you are congratulating someone—after a speech or an award presentation, when you make successful negotiations, etc., you shake hands with others. A handshake is such a practical and friendly way of greeting people that it is universally adopted in all business situations.

5. Situations in Which Handshakes Are Not Needed

Since there are no rules without exceptions, there ARE some situations in which we do NOT extend our hand to shake others': when the other person has his or her hands full, when your hands are not clean enough because of some manual labor, when the person you want to greet is someone much higher ranked than you and to whom you really have nothing to say (In this case, it would look pushy for you to rush up to shake his hand. If, however, the person of much higher rank offers his/her hand first, you certainly should enthusiastically and respectfully extend yours to have a shake), and so on.

II. GENERAL TIPS ON HANDSHAKING

1. If Someone Doesn't See Your Hand Extended

If someone doesn't see your hand extended and doesn't offer his or her hand to you, just draw back your hand and smile.

2. When You Have Cold or Clammy Hands

If you have a tendency to have cold hands, stick your right hand in your jacket pocket to warm it up as you approach a situation in which you'll be shaking hands. Don't hold iced drinks in your right hand. Hold them in your left hand so that your shaking hand is nice and dry. If you have perennially clammy hands, before you shake someone else's hand, give a quick wipe of your right hand on your skirt or trousers, so that when you present it, it's dry. You can do it very quickly and gracefully, no one will be aware that you make the gesture.

3. Points of Protocol in Handshaking

- If you enter a group, shake hands first with your host.

- Shake hands with the host again when you leave. Sometimes this is not possible as when the host of your gathering is surrounded by people and it would be rude for you to interrupt. Use your common sense. If you can easily get to the host to thank him for the meeting, social event, or whatever, fine, shake his hand in goodbye. If you can't easily get to him, leave and telephone him next day or leave a note for him to give your thanks.

- In western society, when a lady meets a gentleman, it is tradition that the lady offers her hand first. After the woman extends her right hand, the man will gently hold the four fingers and make a shake and let go of the fingers.

Section Three Business Card

Business cards play a very important role in trade. They serve as a means of introduction and as a way to ensure that your acquaintance can at a glance collect—and later refer to—your professional details. Given the fact that most companies spend a great deal of time and money designing their business cards, it makes sense to treat them as an effective business tool.

I. DESIGN OF A BUSINESS CARD

Although there are countless distinctive designs of business cards, they basically include such details as name, rank, company and contact information (e.g. telephone number, fax number, correspondence address, email, etc.).

In China, many companies have their staff's business cards bilingually designed—one side of the card is in Chinese and the opposite side in English, because English is the most universally used international language. Diplomats of all countries also have their cards designed with their native languages on one side and English on the other.

When traveling abroad for business, if at all possible, one side of the card should be in the native language of the owner and the opposite side in the local language. This conveys that you are considerate, polite and most importantly, that you are aware of—and sensitive to—the nuances of conducting business internationally.

II. EXCHANGING BUSINESS CARDS

1. When to Exchange Business Cards

Informal meetings are one of the best times to network and exchange business cards. Business cards are generally exchanged at the beginning of or at the end of the meeting. You should wait for the opportunity to come up naturally, such as when someone specifically asks for it or you are engaged in a conversation about business. If the person you are speaking with seems interested in your product or the service you represent, offer that person a business card. Do not mistake the salutary or polite question about what you do as a good opportunity; the card will probably be thrown away if the recipient lacks genuine interest when receiving it.

2. How to Exchange Business Cards

Handing Your Cards to Others

Presenting a card with two hands conveys respect. When using both hands, hold your card by the two upper corners. This way the recipient can conveniently read your card, not receiving an upside-down one.

Good business etiquette requires you present the card so the recipient's language is face up.

Take your time while handing your card to people. It is impossible to convey respect if you simply toss your card at someone—you will come across as being brash and rude. In many countries, it is considered an insult for a guest to be the first to offer a business card.

Accepting a Business Card

When you receive a business card from someone else, make a point of studying any business card, commenting on it and clarifying information before putting it away: Pause and take time to read it; ask any questions that the card itself may bring to mind and comment on the design if practical (The idea is to show interest in any contact's card, which will make them more likely to be interested in yours); use the opportunity to repeat the person's name out loud, especially if it is in a language you're not familiar with—you will be corrected if your pronunciation is off the mark.

Treat cards with respect when receiving them. "Act as though you have received a gift."

Place the business card you receive in a planner or notebook or on the table in front of you. Never place the card in a wallet that will be put in your back pocket. If you don't have a card case with you, put your cards in a front or side pocket.

III. DOS AND DON'TS

Exchanging business cards can be a smooth transaction, or it could be an awkward situation. Use this guide to plan ahead so that you are ready when someone asks for your business card.

1. Do Be Prepared

Always have a handful with you to present to potential clients or other business associates, even on the weekends. You'll find that many important contacts and business card exchanges can take place in the most unlikely places.

Make sure you are carrying more cards than you will need. In some countries, you will need two for each one-to-one visit, as it is customary for the secretary to keep one card.

2. Don't Hand Out Torn or Worn Business Cards

Make sure your cards are clean and crisp with no frayed edges or pen marks. It is not worth saving a few pennies to hand out wrinkled, stained, or torn cards. The best method of keeping your cards in neat form is a business card case. Your business cards should also be up-to-date. Likewise if any of your information has changed: "Business cards with words scratched out gives the impression of disorganization."

3. Don't Hand Out More Than One Card to a New Contact

Only give one business card to your new contact. Leaving two or three may give the signal that you want them to make contacts for you. Unless a prior agreement is made to exchange more than one card, keep the focus on person-to-person contact.

4. Do Exchange Business Cards Smoothly

When you first meet someone, it's ok to request a business card from them provided you have offered yours first. If the person is of a higher position than yourself, you should wait for them to offer their card to you first. Remember if they want you to have a card, they will give you one!

Do not force your card on those who have not asked for it.

5. Do Take Advantage of Free Advertising

Local restaurants often hang a bulletin board near the front counter for business cards to be posted. You can also place your business card in the collection cups for drawings or mixers. They're offering you free advertising, so be ready to take advantage.

6. Do Not Enclose Business Cards in Personal or Emotional Correspondence.

Condolences, "get-well-soons", and even congratulations should be handwritten with no business card accompanying it. These types of correspondences need to show care and time spent by handwriting, and a business card along with it almost seems to say "enough about you, now about me."

7. Never Write on Someone Else's Business Card

It shows a lack of respect for the owner of the card.

Exercises

I. Discussion

1. How will you introduce your roommate to your foreign teacher?

2. First practice the following dialogue in pair and then think about the function of business cards suggested in the dialogue. What other functions do you think business cards have?

Chris: I've been looking forward to this reception for weeks. I can't wait to get some of my own leads. You know, start making new connections.

Nora: Smart thinking. But what are you going to do with all those brochures?

Chris: The party ends at two. I figure I can have them all distributed by one-thirty.

Nora: No, no, no, no. Let me clue you in. Those brochures will make you look like a green hand.

Chris: What should I do then?

Nora: Hand out **business cards**. That's the way to do it.

Chris: I don't understand what's wrong with these brochures about our company.

Nora: This room is going to be filled with potential clients, but there is an unwritten law: you leave your work at the door.

Chris: But how am I supposed to get anything out of this if we can't talk business?

Nora: You have **business cards**. Get out there and exchange cards. Just get a card for a card.

Chris: Then follow up on Monday?

Nora: You catch on quick. Let's split up so we can cover more ground.

Chris: Great idea. This is going to be a piece of cake. I'll meet you back here at two.

II. Designing Practice

Design a business card for you after 10 years, with both Chinese and English language on it.

III. Writing Practice

Write a short self-introduction speech for yourself at an international business conference.

IV. Situational Role-Play

Work in groups to create situations in which you can make introductions, including self-introduction, and create and solve some problems during the introduction. Practice shaking hands and exchanging business cards after the introductions in the same situations.

V. Card Game

First look at the following cards carefully. Then choose one of them and memorize the information on it. Then answer the following questions.

1. Where is the name of the organization located? At the top, bottom, left side, right side, centre?

2. Is there any italic type on the card? If yes, what information is typed in italic font?
3. What is the email address?
4. What is the postal address of the organization?
5. What languages does the card design use? Do you know why?

Sample Card 1

IBM

Full Name

Staff Software Engineer
China System & Technology Lab

IBM (China) Investment Co Limited
Shanghai Branch
Building 10, 399 Keyuan Road,
Zhangjiang Hi-Tech Park, Pudong
New District, Shanghai 201000, China

Tel : (86-21) **00000000**
Fax: (86-21) **00000000**
E-mail: aaaaaa@ibm.com

IBM

姓名

资深软件工程师
中国系统与科技实验室

国际商业机器(中国)投资有限公司
上海分公司
上海市浦东新区张江高科技园区
科苑路399号10号楼
邮编 201000

电话.(86-21) 00000000
传真.(86-21) 00000000
电子邮件: aaaaaa@ibm.com

Sample Card 2

Full Name
Director

Airports Planning Division

Bldg **000** - Zone Sud - Orly Sud **000-00000** ORLY AEROGARE CEDEX (France)
Tel. : **+33 0 00 00 00 00** - **+33 0 00 00 00 00** - Fax : **+33 0 00 00 00 00**
E-mail : **aaabbbccc@adp.fr**

Full Name
Directeur

Direction de l'Aménagement et des Programmes

Bât. **000** - Zone Sud - Orly Sud **000-00000**   ORLY AEROGARE CEDEX
Tél **00 00 00 00 00 - 00 00 00 00 00**   - Télécopie **00 00 00 00 00**
Courriel **aaabbbccc@adp.fr**

Sample Card 3

รองปลัดกระทรวง

กระทรวงการต่างประเทศ   โทร.   000-0000

000 ถนนศรีอยุธยา   000-0000 ต่อ 0000

กรุงเทพฯ 00000   โทรสาร 000-0000

Full Name

DEPUTY PERMANENT SECRETARY

MINISTRY OF FOREIGN AFFAIRS   TEL.000-0000

000 SRI AYUDHYA ROAD,   000-0000 EXT. 0000

BANGKOK 00000, THAILAND   FAX.000-0000

Chapter IV

Visiting and Receiving

When you leave the office to visit customers, colleagues and other associates, your behavior reflects not only on you but on the people you're visiting. And how you handle visitors in your own office speaks volumes about your social skills.

Section One Office Visiting and Receiving

I. VISITING

1. Preparation

- Make an appointment and be punctual.
- Look up your destination on a map before departing.
- Don't bring any food or drinks with you to someone else's office, unless you've been asked to provide food for the meeting.

2. The Visiting

- Be polite to everyone at the office.
- Sit only when invited to do so.
- Don't touch things in someone's office without asking, even if they look like toys.
- Don't read any document, letter, card, etc. on someone else's desk unless given to you.
- If you are only 5 minutes late, it may start an appointment at a wrong foot, so apologize sincerely.
- If your host must take a phone while you are sitting there, ask if he would like privacy for the call "Should I go outside?" If he says no, stay where you are.

  If You Are Kept Waiting
- Do not make demands of the secretary or receptionist while you are waiting.
- Do not take it out on the secretary or receptionist while you are kept waiting.

3. When It Is Time for You to Leave

Whether you accomplished your mission or not during the appointment, thank your host for having received you, shake hands and leave promptly when it is time for you to finish.

4. Follow Up

Write a thank-you letter to the host to show your thankfulness of his/her reception and suggest him/her to visit your company sometime. If necessary, write another follow-up letter to continue to discuss over the things you planned to but have not discussed.

II. RECEIVING

Some people seem to move with fluid grace whether they are entering an elevator, getting out of the cab, or coming into someone's office: they are at ease, and if you watch them closely, you'll find they move efficiently and quietly, inconspicuously. It takes time to practice the skill through careful observation of others, but it also requires a certain amount of unselfishness. They know what to do, but their movements also show they are considerate of others.

A polished business person gives priority attention to how people are received in his or her office.

1. Preparation

- Provide clear direction.
- Be on time with your appointments—if you care about how people perceive you.
- Make sure your documents are ready.
- Clear a comfortable space for your visitors to sit, as well as some writing space on the desk, if needed, especially if your office is a "pile file."
- If you're expecting a group of people, be prepared with sufficient chairs already in place.
- Make your time limitation clear up front.

2. Hosting

- Always stand up to greet and shake hands with visitors entering your office. Move from behind your desk and sit at the same side as your visitor.
- If you are on the telephone when your appointment arrives, terminate the conversation immediately, and say you'll call back later to finish the business at hand.
- Allow your office visitors to be seated before you are.
- Offer your visitors something to drink, such as water, coffee, etc.
- Accept only emergency phone calls and concentrate on your visitors as they shouldn't be made to feel secondary to telephone callers.

• Escort your visitors out instead of letting them wander, especially if your office layout is confusing.

If You Have to Keep Your Visitors Waiting

If you keep someone waiting, he or she will resent it, particularly if that person feels as being forgotten. If you have to, however, follow the guide below:

If you know you're going to keep somebody waiting for over 5 minutes, go out to the reception and apologize.

• A person with an appointment needs special treatment if kept waiting at your office. Sometimes, a series of emergencies will play havoc with your schedule. If you are keeping someone waiting for more than ten minutes, take another minute to leave your office and go to greet your appointment, shake his hand and apologize for the delay, (this will help soothe the angst that may be festering in the heart of an impatient person who hates to be kept waiting). It is particularly grievous when he has had a long-standing appointment with you and has come from far away or when he thinks he is more important than you.

• It's acceptable to give your visitor the opinion of another appointment, which in most cases he will reject.

• Hope you are going to meet your obligation to him soon. Instruct your secretary or assistant to check with you every ten minutes and to report back to him: "It won't be long now. They've almost finished." A comforting smile will help, too. What a waiting person hates most is to be forgotten and to have the receptionist or secretary ignore him and act as though they couldn't care less about his dilemma.

• When you finally are able to receive your visitor, apologize again with sincerity, explain the nature of the emergency, and give him your undivided attention. "Undivided attention" means that you do not take telephone calls during the visit. Staff members may not interrupt you with papers to sign or questions to answer.

• If other visitor has no appointment and is just calling on you for an informal discussion or to sell his products, he will be accustomed to having to wait. He should be treated with respect, however—a comfortable place to sit, something interesting to read (recent magazines, today's newspapers) and, of course, the company's annual report and special publications. Many offices offer refreshment—coffee or a cold drink.

Carefully Get Someone to Leave Your Office

It's important to be gracious, alert, and organized. When you are the busiest you could be, a friend drops in and takes too much time, or an important customer comes in and wants a large dose of premium treatment, screen the visitors.

At a certain moment, look at the clock or watch, and gasp with controlled horror "Good Lord, it's eleven o'clock! I have a meeting coming up right now." Rise quickly from your chair, flushed with the recognition of a real emergency at hand. Your visitor will rise too. Put out your hand, shake his warmly, and then apologize for having to finish the appointment so abruptly: "Please write me a letter concerning anything we haven't discussed." While offering your hand, you're also leading him to the coat closet or the exit door. Never be embarrassed about ending a meeting that has had its allotted time.

3. Seeing the Visitors Off

When bidding farewell to a visitor in your office, it is good manner to open the door and go out after him or her. It is usual, then, to escort him or her to a point of exit from the company. This may be to the elevator, to the gate of your company's building, to the parking lot, or even to a bus stop. In some companies, to go with the guest to the company's gate is required.

III. THE RECEPTIONIST

The treatment afforded to a visitor by your company's receptionist (who may be primarily someone's secretary stationed near the office entrance) is as important as the first voice a caller hears upon phoning your office. The welcome should be warm and efficient. A receptionist should understand the importance of the job as keeper of the gate and the voice of the company greeting the public.

If one can be familiar enough with the following checklist mainly made by Professor Yang Junfeng, he or she can surely be a capable receptionist:

Behavior Guides for the Receptionist

A receptionist should:

- dress conservatively;
- wear makeup properly (if a lady, usually a lady) and have his/her hairstyle neatly and conservatively done, but not fuss with his/her face or his/her hair once he/ she is on the job;
- wear little jewelry, and what he/she does wear is noiseless and unobtrusive;
- not eat, chew gum, smoke, or drink at the receptionist desk;
- not read newspaper at the desk, since they are so messy;
- read either magazines or a book hidden on the lap—and only when there is no activity in the area over which he/she is presiding;
- keep hands and fingernails presentable;
- keep the desk neat, with everything in its proper place;
- make sure that the reception area is clean at all times and equipped with good company reading materials, including company product catalogs, annual reports

and so on;

- smile when greeting each visitor, and his/her conduct and behavior show he/she is glad to see each one, his/her voice is cheerful when he/she uses the telephone to announce the visitor;

- transmit orders and directions to the visitor in a very dear manner so that she can be easily understood;

- not make personal calls of any length while on the job;

- never continues a conversation he/she is having when a visitor approaches the desk unless it is an important one; when on the telephone, not turn her back to the visitor as though trying to shut him out;

- call to see what is happening and then reports to the visitor if a visitor is kept waiting longer than usual;

- treat executives, visitors, and employees with equal courtesy as they enter and leave his/her area;

- call everyone by his or her last name, so that the reception area has an air of dignity;

- fastidiously keep the company directory up to date, with accurate names, numbers and locations of all personnel;

- know senior management—their titles, what they do, and how they fit into the hierarchy—so he/she can intelligently answer any question asked by a visitor;

- make sure his/her area has everything it needs, including a guest telephone, sufficient closet space, an umbrella stand, etc. as well as the proper sign-in book, if signing-in is company policy for security's sake.

Section Two Business Trip and Receiving Visitors from Another City or Another Country

In international business, visiting and receiving do not only take place in an office or in the same city. There are more and more opportunities when business people go on a trip to pay a business visit on companies in another city or another country. And the host tends to arrange a relatively ceremonious reception since the visitor is from a place far away.

I. BUSINESS TRIP

1. Preparation

List a checklist of the activities during your visit.

Search some information about the city and/or the country you are going to visit.

Make air tickets and hotel room booking.

By email or fax, make confirmation with the company you are going to visit, about all the activities that you are going to participate in during your stay, including your accommodation arrangement (sometimes your passport or ID No. will be needed).

Inquire the host about any special preparations you need to make for the visit.

Prepare at least three different sets of outfits: business suit for the business visit, conference or negotiation, evening dress for formal occasions such as the reception dinner and the welcome ceremony and casual wear for relaxation and entertainment.

Prepare gifts for the host and the person who is in charge of your visit. If the host is a person who has built such a long and credible relationship with you that you have become friends, be prepared to pay a visit to his/her family and prepare gifts for the family members.

Take some regular OTC medicine with you, just in case.

2. Visiting

The No. 1 basic rule is to follow the plan and respect the arrangement of the host. If there is misunderstanding, inefficiency or difference from the original plan, remember that your purpose is to achieve something, but not to find fault. Harboring resentment or turning out to the reception staff will not help solve the problem, only harming your relationships.

The second rule is to remain professional. Although you are on a trip and may be relatively relaxed, you are still at work! And remember that you pay the visit on behalf of your company, not yourself, so your behavior reflects not only on your personality, but also the image of your company.

Be thoughtful and sincere—thoughtful enough to keep in mind that the host is trying the best to entertain you and be grateful to the host for what he/she has done for you, and sincere enough to make the other side believe their effort is rewarding. This way you can enjoy your visit and stay to the utmost extent.

3. Departure

Before you leave, there may be a reception dinner to see you off. At the dinner, it is thoughtful for you to make it a big event to sincerely express that you are grateful to your host for the warm welcome, considerate arrangement, etc, and that you hope you will have the opportunity of reciprocating. In fact, at this dinner, the host probably has already seen you off. On departure, therefore, get all your belongings well packed and bother the host as little as possible. The host may be your company till you get aboard the plane or the train. Sometimes the host is also likely to arrange somebody, on his/her behalf (and you will be informed of this beforehand), to help you check out of the hotel, and see you off at the airport or railway station, helping you with your luggage and the check-in there. Make an appointment with the person and be on time. Do not keep him/her waiting. Sincerely thank the person who helps you out with your departure.

4. Follow Up

Write a letter to say that you have returned home safe and sound, and, again, express your gratefulness to the host's reception, how much you have enjoyed the visit there, and you are looking forward to opportunities of reciprocating his/her courtesy; finally, in your letter, suggest him/her to pay a visit to your place. Write a thank-you note to the person who sees you off on behalf of the host if there is one.

II. RECEIVING VISITORS FROM ANOTHER CITY OR ANOTHER COUNTRY

1. Preparation

Maybe you are in the front-line as far as public relations are concerned. You are often involved in receiving visitors from other parts of the country or even from overseas. Careful preparation such as booking hotel and arranging reception dinner must be made and a checklist of the activities required needs to be drawn up. It is also helpful if you do a little discreet background research on the distinguished guests.

The visitor will have a plan for the coming trip. In this case, one week before the visitor's arriving date, you should check with him/her by emails and/or FAX to confirm the date of his/her arrival and the exact arrival time of the plane or train the visitor is going to take, and inquire about the special needs of the visitor during the stay that need to be arranged beforehand.

2. Hosting

Receiving the Visitor at the Airport/Railway Station

Compared with the small effort invested, the effect of welcoming people personally on their arrival at the airport can be highly rewarding. When you go to the airport to receive visitors, you should pay attention to the following points:

- Approaching the person you are meeting;
- Inquiring about their journey;
- Offering help with their luggage;
- Suggest leaving.

Inquire whether any other help is needed and if he or she has a particular concern at the moment: return bookings; money exchange; calling home. When all this has been settled, his or her mind will be much more receptive to your intended tour of the beauties of the town (徐小贞, 2005).

In addition, you should note that your dress is also important.

Since the accommodation has already been arranged ahead of time, when the visitor arrives at the hotel, you may leave, so that the visitor can have a good rest after the long journey. Leave enough time for the visitors before you come into real business (at least one day), because some visitors who come from overseas need a good rest to get over the jet leg and adjust to the new location and time zone. Settle down the meeting time and talk about your business itinerary then.

Reception Dinner

There is always at least one formal reception dinner, either for welcome or for farewell. Inform the visitor of the time, venue, the diners and the degree of formality of the dinner, so that the visitor can make corresponding preparation for it. For example, the visitor will probably want to know whether the dinner is formal or not, so that he/she can dress himself/herself properly. When the time of the dinner is due, meet the visitor at the lobby of the hotel he/she lives at and lead him/her to the very venue lest he/she should get lost in a city that is not familiar to him/her.

For dining etiquette part, please see Chapter Five.

Take the guest back to the hotel after the dinner.

Other Entertaining

Besides talking business and visiting the company, the host is also expected to entertain the visitor in a relaxing way, such as arranging one to two days' sightseeing around the city.

3. Bidding Farewell to the Visitors

If you are in charge of seeing off a visitor from a faraway place, you are expected to see him or her off at the airport or the railway station and not to leave him/her until he or she has caught the train, plane or boat and is finally out of sight. Before the visitor's departure day, call him/her at hotel to confirm the leaving time and flight number and inquire whether he/she has some special needs, such as arrangement of transportation. On the departure day, meet the visitor at hotel, accompanying him/her to the airport or the railway station, and help your guest with his/her luggage and the boarding procedure. Take good control of time, because there is always a long period time allotted for the check-in, and do not miss the flight or the train.

Remember to bring a souvenir as a small gift to the visitor and wish him/her a safe and sound journey. Of course, on behalf of both you and your company, express that you are looking forward to his/her visiting again or you are looking forward to meeting him/her again.

Table Manners

● Have you seen the movie "Titanic"? Besides the touching love story, what did you get from it? Have you learned anything about table manners? Let's look back on this classic movie.

[Jack is invited to dinner by Rose's fiancé. Before Jack goes to the dining room, he meets a friendly old lady, Molly.]

Molly: Uh son? Son, do you have the slightest comprehension of what you're doing?

Jack: Not really.

Molly: Well, you're about to go into the snake pit. What are you planning to wear?

[Jack gestures towards the shabby clothes he is wearing]

[Molly sniffs, shakes her head and laughs kindly]

Molly: I figured so. Come on.

[In Molly's stateroom, men's suits and jackets and formal wear are strewn all over the place. Jack is well-dressed.]

Molly: I was right. You and my son are just about the same size.

Jack: Pretty close.

Molly [whistles]: You shine up like a new penny.

Cut to

[Jack comes to the elegant dining hall. He imitates the moves and gestures of the gentlemen around him and tries to be one of them.]

[Rose shows up in an evening dress.]

Jack: [gently lifts Rose's hand and kisses it] I saw that in a nickelodeon once and I always wanted to do it.

[Rose laughs. Jack raised his right arm and Rose holds it.]

Rose: [walks with Jack to her mother and her fiancé Carl] Darling, surely you remember Mr. Dawson.

Carl: [surprised] Dawson, why, it's a-mazing, you could almost pass for a gentle-man.

Jack: Almost.

Carl: Extraordinary.

......

[All the people are seated. Rose sits across the table from Jack. She secretly shows Jack how to use the napkin.]

Jack: [looking at his silverware, confused]

[He whispers to Molly, who is on his right.]Are these all for me?

Molly: Just start from the outside and work your way in.

Waiter: How do you take your caviar, sir?

Jack: No caviar for me, thanks. Never did I like it much.

● **Do you know any other Hollywood movies from which you learned some table manners? Please illustrate these table manners in details.**

Like it or not, table manners stand out as perhaps the single most important benchmark of etiquette. Table manners give us confidence by providing guidelines on what to do during this very public and rather gross activity. Of course, confidence is the name of the game when it comes to building strong relationships with people—and having confidence in your table manners as you eat is one of the surest ways to make a positive impact on your dining companions.

Good table manners are critical for another related reason as well: The reality is, people judge other people by their table manners. In a business situation, table manners may well be the key factor that differentiates you from your competition. This chapter is designed to help you know as much as possible about how to deal with dining situations in the business world.

Section One   Arriving for Dinner

I. A GUEST'S PRE-PLANNING

As a guest to a business dinner, the impression you make on your business meal companions starts when you first arrive, well before you lift your first utensil.

1. If you are invited out for dinner, make an effort with your appearance. It shows a reciprocation of effort. If you are uncertain of the dress code, check with your hosts.

2. When dinner is stated as, 8:00 or 8:30 p.m., it's most polite to arrive within 10—15 minutes of the earliest stated time. It gives you time to say hello to the hosts, meet the other guests, and settle in with a drink. Do not arrive early. Not only is it rude, but it is also a pain in the butt. You'll only get in the way of the final preparations of either the food or the host.

3. Should you be running more than 15 minutes late, ring the hostess letting her know of your delay. Dinner is traditionally held off for no longer than 15 to 20 minutes to avoid it being spoiled.

4. At less formal dinners, bringing a bottle of wine or chocolate is considered a thoughtful gesture. Etiquette states what is brought ought to be something one doesn't need. Avoid bringing flowers to a big dinner party. It is inconvenient for the hostess who has to extract herself from welcoming guests and go hunting for a vase.

5. At a very formal dinner, it is incorrect to bring a gift at all.

II. SEATING PROTOCOL

Approaching the table, a guest always looks to the host/hostess for seating assignments.

At a formal dinner, there will usually be a seating plan near the door of the dining room, or place cards on the table. If neither exists, the guest should wait to be seated by the host/hostess, who may have a specific seating arrangement in mind.

Though appointing the seating for the guests may seem stuffy, it generally puts guests at ease. People like to know where the host wants them to sit and will often ask before being seated if the place they have chosen is all right.

Therefore, if you are the one who take charge of the seating arrangement, there are a few simple rules that apply to most situations:

1. When there is but a single table, the host and hostess usually sit at opposite ends, or occasionally in the center of the table facing each other. When multiple tables are needed, the host and hostess may be at separate tables in which case you may wish to opt for a co-host and co-hostess.

2. Generally, when the event involves both men and women, guests are seated alternating man and woman. The place of honor is to the right of the host if the guest is a woman, and to the right of the hostess if the guest is a man. That is to say, the highest ranking male generally sits to the right of the hostess. The wife of the highest ranking man or the highest ranking woman herself sits to the right of the host. Guests are then seated alternating left to right from the host and hostess after the honored guest is seated. The second ranking male will usually sit to the left of the hostess. Now the seating should be arranged such that no two women sit side by side and no two men sit side by side.

3. This will prove a difficult feat when the number of guests is evenly divisible by four, so try to avoid this possibility. Should it happen, however, the male guest of honor may sit across from the host in the hostess' seat. The hostess then sits to his left.

4. Spouses who do not hold positions themselves are seated according to the rank of their husbands or wives. It is often preferable to avoid seating husbands and wives together, but many wives may be more comfortable if seated together with their husbands.

5. The key here is to be practical. Don't seat two people who notoriously get into vicious arguments next to each other just to fit a boy-girl, boy-girl seating arrangement.

6. If a guest objects to the seating you have chosen, simply make a quick change.

7. In traditional socializing, the purpose of this seating arrangement of alternating man and woman is that every lady could communicate with and be taken care of by a gentleman. Business dinners, however, do not always involve men and women equal in numbers. Sometimes they are gatherings of business persons of either sex from two or more companies or different countries. In those cases, it is acceptable to arrange the host's seat facing the door and then "alternate host and guest", that is to say, each guest sits next to the host or a representative of the host so that they can communicate. Besides, diners' rankings should also be taken into consideration.

To visualize how guests would be seated, please look at the following Seating Diagrams.

1. The most traditional arrangement calls for the host and hostess to sit at the two ends of the table. (The horizontal straight line through the center of the table is the virtual symmetry axis)

HOSTESS

MAN	1	2	MAN
WOMAN	3	4	WOMAN
MAN	5	6	MAN
WOMAN	6	5	WOMAN
MAN	4	3	MAN
WOMAN	2	1	WOMAN

HOST

2. Whenever the total number of people at table equals any multiple of four and there is an equal number of men and women, to balance the table, the hostess simply moves one seat to the left, thereby putting her right-hand guest (guest of honor) opposite to the host.

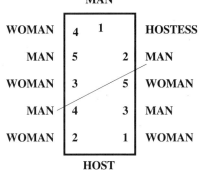

(1) Multiples of four—rectangular table (couples all married)

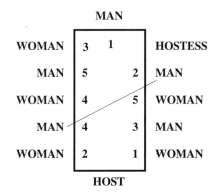

(2) Multiples of four—rectangular table (Man 4 and Woman 4 are not a married couple)

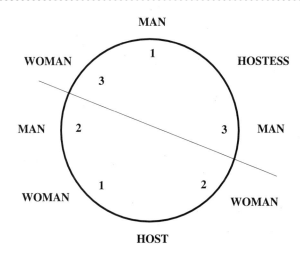

(3) Multiples of four—round table (all couples married)

3. Business reception—round table: Company A is the host company. The Arabic number 1 stands for highest ranking, and then 2, 3, 4.

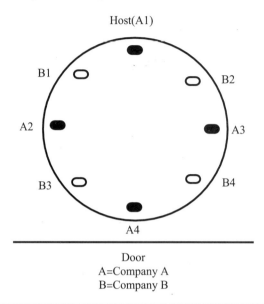

Host(A1)

A=Company A
B=Company B

4. Seating arrangement of a governmental reception dinner for APEC Senior Officials: At the dinner, the seat of the host, the governor, faces the door and each guest neighbors the governor, a vice governor, a department chief or a mayor of the city of a province. The Arabic numbers here do not stand for rankings of different levels, but different countries, departments or cities.

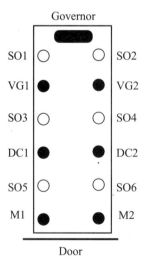

SO=Senior Official
VG=Vice Governor
M=Mayor

APEC: Asia-Pacific Economic Cooperation

The Guest of Honor

The guest of honor refers to the guest who deserves the honor, or who the host/hostess defers to. How do you decide who you should give the honors to?

Suppose you are the host/hostess, and you are with the boss/his or her spouse, he/she gets the honors; if you are with an older man/woman, he/she receives the honors; if you are with a senior man/woman in any way, give him/her the honors. If you simply don't know what to do, just remember that no one would ever consider you rude for honoring them in some way, so be gracious and give the other men/women the honors.

Section Two Placing Orders

I. AT A RESTAURANT

When you go out for a business dinner, follow the four pieces of advice from Ms Peggy Post (2005):

At a restaurant, once you are settled in your seat, you can expect a waiter to come to the table to take drink orders. The waiter may also bring menus if the food hasn't already been ordered for you.

1. When the Waiter Asks for Your Drink Orders

<u>When you are asked first</u>, as a junior executive at the table, you don't know if you should order alcohol or not. In this situation, err on the side of safety and order something non-alcoholic. If others, including your boss, order an alcoholic drink, you can either quietly change your order before the server leaves the table or opt not to have alcohol before the meal. Either choice is appropriate.

2. When the Waiter Asks for Your Food Order

As you look over the menu, keep in mind three important guidelines to ordering:

• Order medium-priced dishes, not the most expensive items on the menu.
• Know the food you are ordering. This isn't the time to be adventuresome and order something you've never had before. Not only might you not like it, but also it might be difficult to eat. You want your focus to be on the people at the table and not on your food.
• Order food that is relatively easy to eat. Linguine with clam sauce is very tasty, but eating linguine is a challenge that's nearly certain to leave your tie or blouse spattered with sauce.

3. What if the menu is pre-arranged and you have a special dietary need?

If, for instance, you are a vegetarian, it is perfectly acceptable to quietly ask the waiter whether there is a vegetarian selection available. If there isn't, you can ask him or her to bring you a plate without the meat on it. The key is to make your request known without making a big deal out of it.

4. Is there anything you have to order?

As you listen to the other people ordering, you realize they are all having an appetizer, a salad, and a main course—while all you want is a main course. There is no requirement for you to order any course you don't want. Simply order the main course and politely say "No, thank you" if you are asked whether you want anything else.

II. DECODING THE MENU

In its simplest form, a dinner can consist of three or four courses, such as soup, salad, meat and dessert. Under no circumstances would a private dinner, no matter how formal, consist of more than Hors d'oeuvre, Soup, Entrée, Roast, Salad, Dessert and Coffee in this order. In formal dining, however, a full course dinner can consist of eight, ten or twelve courses, and, in its extreme form, has been known to have twenty-one courses.

1. Starters

APPETIZERS

Hors d'oeuvre or appetizers are served before the main courses of a meal.

If there is an extended period between when guests arrive and when the meal is served (for example, during a cocktail hour), these might also serve the purpose of sustaining guests during the wait. Hors d'oeuvre is sometimes served with no meal served afterward. This is the case with many reception and cocktail party events.

Hors d'oeuvre might include: Canapés, Cold cuts, Crudités, Snack foods, Cheeses, Sausages and Dumplings.

SOUP

Traditionally, soups are classified into two broad groups: *clear soups* and *thick soups*.

The established French classifications of clear soups are *bouillon* and *consommé*.

Thick soups are classified depending upon the type of thickening agent used: *purées* are vegetable soups thickened with starch; *bisques* are made from puréed shellfish thickened with *cream*; cream soups are thickened with béchamel sauce; and *veloutés* are thickened with eggs, butter and cream.

Cold soups are a particular variation on the traditional soup, wherein the temperature when served is kept at or below room temperature. In summer, they can form part of a dessert tray.

Fruit soups are served hot or cold depending on the recipe. Many recipes are for cold soups served when fruit is in season during hot weather. Fruit soups may include milk, sweet or savory dumplings, spices, or alcoholic beverages like brandy or champagne.

SALAD

The salad course refers to service of any green vegetable, although it is commonly thought of as involving lettuce. This course is formally after the main course, but regional tradition may be to serve it just before the main course (like in North America).

Popular types of garden salads are: Caesar salad, Chef Salad, Chinese chicken salad, Cobb salad, Greek salad, Michigan salad.

ENTREE

Its traditional definition, still used almost everywhere in the world outside of North America, refers to a smaller course that precedes the main course; however, in North America, the disappearance in the early 20th century of a large communal main course such as a roast as a standard part of the meal has led to the term being used to describe the main course itself.

2. Main Course

A main course is the featured or primary dish in a meal consisting of several courses. It is sometimes called the meat course.

The main course is usually the heaviest, heartiest, and most complex or substantial dish on a menu. The main ingredient is usually meat or fish; in vegetarian meals, the main course sometimes attempts to mimic a meat course.

In formal dining, a well-planned main course can function as a sort of gastronomic apex or climax. In such a scheme, the preceding courses are designed to prepare for and lead up to the main course in such a way that the main course is anticipated and, when the scheme is successful, increased in its ability to satisfy and delight the diner. The courses following the main course then calm the palate and the stomach, acting as a sort of denouement or anticlimax.

The main course is most often preceded by an appetizer, soup, or salad, and followed by salad and a dessert.

3. Dessert

A dessert typically comes at the end of a meal, usually consisting of sweet food, sometimes with a strong flavor, such as some cheeses. Common desserts include cakes, cookies, fruits, pastries, ice cream, and candies.

> The word *dessert* is most commonly used for this course in U.S., Canada, Australia, and Ireland, while *sweet*, *pudding* or *afters* would be more typical terms in the UK and some other Commonwealth countries, including India. *Pudding* is the proper term, *dessert* is only to be used if the course consists of fruit, and *sweet* and *afters* are colloquial. In colloquial American usage *dessert* has a broader meaning and can refer to anything sweet that follows a meal, including milkshakes and other beverages.

Some have a separate final sweet course but others mix sweet and savory dishes throughout the meal as in Chinese cuisine, or reserve elaborate dessert concoctions for special occasions. Often, the dessert is seen as a separate meal or snack rather than a course, and may be eaten apart from the meal (usually in less formal settings). Some restaurants specialize in dessert.

4. Wines Matching Dishes

The old advice on selecting a wine is to stick with white wines for *white meats* and red wines with *red meats*. Today, the recommendation of each is based less on color than on the balance of sweetness and acidity that makes for a food-friendly wine.

> In gastronomy, red meat is darker-colored meat, as contrasted with white meat. The exact definition varies by time, place, and culture, but the meat of adult mammals such as cows, sheep, and horses is invariably considered red, while chicken and rabbit are invariably considered white. The meat of young mammals, such as milk-fed veal, calves and sheep, and pigs is traditionally considered white; while the meat of duck and goose is considered red.

Listed below are wines that generally go well with certain kinds of dishes:

COURSE	WINE
Shellfish or Hors d'oeuvre	Chablis, Graves, Rhine, Moselle
Soup	Sauterne, Dry Sherry, Madeira
Fish	White Bordeaux, White Burgundy, Rhine, Moselle
Roasts / White Meats	White Bordeaux, White Burgundy, Champagne
Fowl or Game	Fine Claret, Red Burgundy, Rhone,
Cheese	Fine Claret, Red Burgundy, Port, Old Sherry, Full-bodied Madeira
Dessert	Madeira, Rich Old Sherry,
Coffee	Cognac, Port, Old Sherry, Madeira, Liqueur

5. A Seven Course Dinner

When a fancy dinner such as a seven course dinner is served, it begins with a cocktail hour in a lounge where guests sip light drinks and consume small appetizers. When everyone is seated for dinner, the seven course dinner begins with an appetizer course.

Guests at a seven course dinner will be offered a choice of thick or clear soup with the soup course.

Fish is usually served on its own, before the meat courses, and guests may be offered poultry, beef, or lamb as a main meat course. Some formal dinners also serve one or more separate vegetable courses, which can act as palate cleansers themselves, to relieve the weightiness of the flesh courses. In general, the food gets heavier as the dinner progresses.

No formal dinner would be complete without dessert. Dessert choices at a seven course dinner might include a cheese plate, a fruit plate, crème brûlée, or a cake course. Desserts are often quite elaborately arranged, and can be decorated with edible flowers, chocolate sculptures, and other edible ornamental accents to draw the eye of the guests.

After dessert, strong liquors such as brandy and fortified dessert wines will be offered, to signal to guests that the meal is over.

A sample seven-course menu is given below:

Seven-Course Menu		
Course Number	Course	Wine
1	Shrimp cocktail, oysters, clams on Chablis, the half shell	Chablis
2	Soup (usually clear)	Sherry
3	Fish (hot or cold. The separate fish course is rarely seen in	Rhine
	the United States. However, it is very common in Europe.)	
4	Main course of meat (usually beef) and vegetables	Claret
	or	
	Main course of game and vegetables	Burgundy
5	Salad	Claret/Burgundy
6	Dessert (ice cream, sherbet)	Champagne
7	Fruit (pears, grapes)	Champagne

Section Three Formal Place Settings

No matter how informal today's entertaining style has become, tradition is still maintained in table customs. There is a wonderful sense of security that comes with knowing what is correct in the order of flatware, where to place the glasses, butter plates and napkins. The traditional placement of these items must be followed for both the hosts and their guests to be comfortable.

At a traditionally formal meal, there is no butter plate, or dessert spoon and fork. Bread traditionally was not served with formal meals, and the dessert fork and spoon would be presented with the finger bowls. Sherry was served with the soup; a dry white wine with the fish. Red wine was served with meat, duck, and game. Champagne was served with dessert. Coffee is served in another room, not the dining room. Here is a diagram of formal place setting.

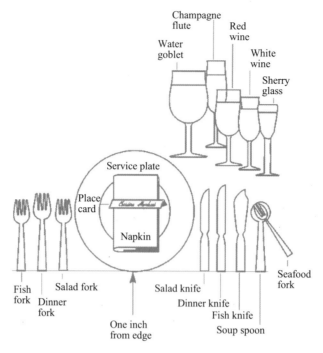

Note that the above setting is the European Style where the salad is eaten at the end. Americans will typically place the salad fork left to the fish fork and the salad knife right to the fish knife. The map below shows you an American formal place setting.

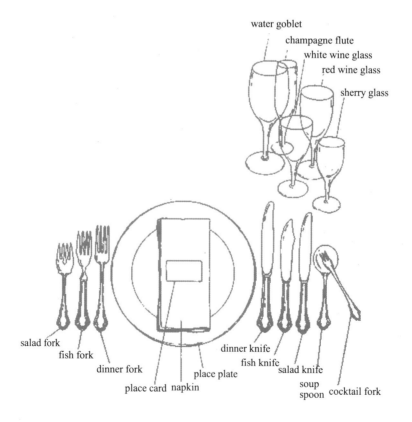

FLATWARE

The flatware is always placed in order of its use, starting from the outside in, moving toward the plate. Forks are placed tines up on the left side of the plate: the fish fork (if there is to be a fish course) to the far left, the dinner fork next and the salad fork next to the plate (European Style). The knives are placed on the right, the one to be used first farthest from the plate, with the sharp edges towards the plate. The soup spoon goes to the right of the knives. Dessert spoons and forks may be placed horizontally above the place setting, (with the spoon facing left and the fork facing right) or they may be brought to the table as the course is served. Butter knives and plates are never a part of the formal table setting. If bread is served, the butter plate should be on the left above the forks and the butter knife is placed diagonally across the butter plate, from the upper left to the lower right. If the menu requires a cocktail/oyster fork, it is placed to the right of the spoon; it is the only fork ever used on the right. No more than three of any implement is ever used in a place setting, so if a fourth fork is needed it should be brought to the table as the course is served. The salad knife may not be needed, as is shown in the following diagram.

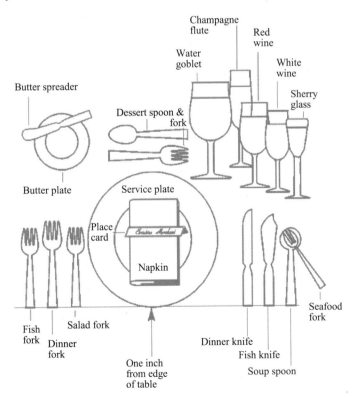

DINNER WARE

Service plates/chargers are usually used in formal place setting. A service plate goes underneath the first course plate; and sometimes under the first two courses. Properly, from the time the table is set until it is cleared for dessert, a plate should remain at each place. The plate on which the shrimp cocktail or other appetizer is served is put on top of the service plate. The soup bowl is also put on the service plate. If the salad were to be served before the main course, the salad plate would also be placed on top of the service plate. When it is time for the main course, the used plate is removed along with the service plate and immediately replaced with the main course plate. After dinner, the plates are removed, leaving the table without plates.

GLASSWARE

The menu determines the glasses used for dinner. The water goblet is directly above the knives or to the right of the plate; at a slight distance to the right is the champagne glass; in front of and between these two glasses is the red wine glass or white wine glass; then further to the right is the sherry glass. Instead of grouping the glasses on the table, some mess personnel place them in a straight row slanting downward from the goblet at the upper left to the sherry glass at the lower right. Each glass is removed with the course it accompanies. The dessert wine glass, however, stays throughout the serving of the demitasse, and only two wines, sherry and champagne may be served.

NAPKINS AND PLACE CARDS

The napkin at a formal dinner is placed on the service plate; if a first course is on the table when the diners sit down, the napkin is placed to the left of the forks.

A flat place card may be placed on top of this napkin. It may also be positioned above the plate on the tablecloth or centered above the service plate. They should be used whenever there are eight or more people.

CUPS AND SAUCERS

If coffee is to be served with the meal, the cup and saucer are placed to the right of the setting with the coffee spoon on the saucer.

SALT AND PEPPER SHAKER

Since more people use salt than pepper (and most people are right-handed), the salt shaker is placed to the right of the pepper shaker, in a position closer to the right hand. Because salt is finer than pepper, the lid of the salt shaker is punctured with smaller, more numerous holes than a pepper shaker.

Section Four   Facing a Formal Dinner Gracefully

All the rules of table manners are made to avoid ugliness. To let anyone see what you have in your mouth is repulsive, to make a noise is to suggest an animal, to make a mess is disgusting.

—Emily Post

Now that you've solved the mysteries of a formal dinner table, you are ready to move on to that most daunting dining dilemma—the formal dinner. You'll be able to handle this challenge with grace and confidence if you know what to expect and how to react.

I. BEFORE EATING

1. Before sitting down

If you have cocktails before dinner, leave them there. Bring them to the table only if the hostess suggests it.

A lipstick trail is the red badge of discourtesy. Take precautions before you reach the table. This is also the time to visit the restroom for hair repair and other finishing touches.

At a formal dinner, the host offers his arm to the female guest of honor, and they go into the dining room. The hostess and her dinner partner, the male guest of honor, enter last.

2. You're seated

Napkins

After you are seated, wait for your host to make the first napkin move. When the host places the napkin on his or her lap, the guests should follow suit. Always remember to follow the lead of your hostess.

Large dinner napkins should remain folded in half and placed across your lap with the fold facing your waist. Never "flap" the napkin to unfold it.

Note that the napkin remains in your lap until after the meal and a piece of cloth around the neck is not a napkin for an adult, but a bib for a little child. Here is a funny but embarrassing story about someone tying his napkin round his neck: A poor man who had never eaten at a luxurious restaurant once won a lot of money, so he decided that he could now afford a holiday in an excellent hotel by the sea. When lunch-time came on his first day there, he decided to go and eat in the restaurant of the hotel. The head waiter showed him to his table, took his order and went away. When he looked at the man again, he had a surprise! The man had tied his table napkin round his neck. The head waiter was very annoyed at this and immediately told one of the other waiters in the restaurant to go to the man and inform him, without being in any way insulting, that people did not do such a thing in restaurants of that quality. The waiter went to the farmer and said in a friendly voice, "Good morning, sir, would you like a shave, or a haircut?"

Posture

Your general posture at the table should be a straight back. When eating, sit close enough to the table so each bite is brought to the mouth without having to lean forward.

Your feet should be firmly planted on the floor in front of you. Do not cross your legs, do not lean back on your chair, and do not shake your feet. Never tip a chair backward; the position is hard on the back chair legs and disturbs the symmetry of the table setting. Avoid wrapping your feet around the legs of the chair. Refrain from extending your legs under the table, putting your arm on the back of a dinner partner's chair, or looping your arm around the back of the chair.

Elbows and forearms off the table

In England, the correct behavior is to keep your hands on your lap when you are not using them. In France the rule is to keep your hands above the table at all times. You may place them on the edge of the table but you must never put your elbows on the table. But between courses, in the interest of hearing conversation at a crowded or noisy table, the elbows are rested on the table so one may lean forward, or the wrist and forearm are placed on the edge of the table.

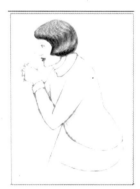

In a noisy atmosphere, to better hear the conversation between courses, rest the elbows on the table and lean forward.

Or, place the wrist and forearm on the edge of the table and lean forward

II. USING EATING UTENSILS PROPERLY

1. Knife and Fork

It is important to hold the fork horizontally by balancing it between the first knuckle of the middle finger and the tip of the index finger while the thumb steadies the handle. The knife on the other hand is used with the tip of the index finger leaning on the blade of the knife. Do not apply too much pressure; simply use it as leverage and guidance, as you cut your food. Just remember to look around if you forget what to do in a particular situation. Just stay calm and enjoy the meal.

2. Spoons

Spoons are for coffee, tea, soup, bouillon, custard, pudding, soft desserts, but not vegetables. Hold the spoon like holding a pencil.

Spoons stir tea or coffee, but don't drink with them. After you have stirred your beverage, remove the spoon from the glass or cup. Place it on the serving plate beneath the glass or on the saucer beneath the cup. It does not go on the table cloth. If the glass does not have a dish under it, place the spoon on your plate.

3. Proper Eating Styles

There are two ways of using a knife and fork to cut and eat your food. They are **the American style** and **the European or Continental style**. Either style is considered appropriate.

In **the American style**, one cuts the food by holding the knife in the right hand and the fork in the left hand with the fork tines piercing the food to secure it on the plate. Cut a few bite-size pieces of food then lay your knife across the top edge of your plate with the sharp edge of the blade facing in. Change your fork from your left to your right hand to eat, fork tines facing up. (If you are left-handed, keep your fork in your left hand, tines facing up.)

The European or Continental style is the same as the American style in that you cut your meat by holding your knife in your right hand while securing your food with your fork in your left hand. The difference is, your fork remains in your left hand, tines facing down, and the knife in your right hand. Simply eat the cut pieces of food by picking them up with your fork still in your left hand.

What is a finger bowl?

The finger bowl is a shallow round bowl (like a china soup bowl), which is placed atop a larger plate (like a big saucer).

Although the finger bowl has all but vanished in current dining rooms, it may infrequently be found in the finest eating establishments. Certain enthusiasts of high cuisine have called for the resurrection of the finger bowl.

Antique hunters may uncover finger bowls, as they search through collections of old china.

How is a finger bowl used?

The finger bowl is filled with warm water.

Often, a lemon wedge is placed on the under plate. Occasionally, lemon wheels are floated in the water itself.

The diner dips his fingers gently into the warm water to rinse them lightly. Splashing, swirling and swishing in the finger bowl are considered improper. The finger bowl is not intended as a bath or cleansing, but merely as a means of preparing the hands for the final courses of the meal.

The finger bowl is usually accompanied by a fresh napkin or cloth, with which the diner may wipe his moistened hands. This cloth is removed by the waiter, along with the finger bowl and underplate.

When is the finger bowl used?

Traditionally, at a fancy restaurant or country club, a finger bowl is presented after the main course.

The finger bowl is set before a diner immediately after his main course plate has been removed.

What is the purpose of the finger bowl?

The idea is for the diner to clean his fingers, particularly after a sticky or messy meal, such as ribs, corn-on-the-cob, fried chicken or shellfish.

Shortly after the finger bowl, a palate-cleansing dish (such as a fruit sorbet) is often introduced. Or the finger bowl may be followed by the dessert or cheese course.

III. When Dinner is served

1. Serving Order

The female guest of honor is served first. All food is served from the left, and all beverages from the right. When being served at a home, the server moves counter clockwise, or to the right.

The server serves with the left hand, and picks up with the right hand. Dishes can be removed from either side.

2. Eating

Holding your hands in front of you, touch the tips of your thumbs to the tips of your forefingers to make a lower case "b" with your left hand and a lower case "d" with your right hand. This reminds you that "bread and butter" go to the left of the place setting and "drinks" go on the right.

When to Start?

When the host/hostess picks up his/her fork, you may pick up yours and begin to eat. Wait until the hostess lifts her fork as the signal to begin eating. If there isn't a hostess, the female guest of honor lifts her fork as the signal. If that doesn't apply, simply wait until everyone is served, and then one of the women (*if there are any*) will pick up her fork, and everyone should follow her lead.

Before the first course arrives, drinks and bread will soon arrive at the table. These mark your first opportunity to deal with food at the same time you are trying to carry on a conversation.

Bread is most often placed on the table in a basket that everyone shares. If the bread is placed in front of you, feel free to pick up the basket and offer it to the person on your left. Then take a piece yourself and pass it to the right.

You place the bread and butter on your butter plate, then break off a bite-sized piece of bread, put a little butter on it, and eat it. Don't butter the whole piece of bread and then take bites from it.

Appetizers

Appetizers are typically eaten with a fork and knife, though in some cases they will be eaten with your fingers. If you do eat food with your fingers, try to take bite-sized pieces rather than bringing a big piece of food to your mouth and then tearing a bite off with your teeth.

Shrimp cocktail typically arrives in a glass with a long stem, set on a small plate. If the shrimp is small enough to be eaten in one bite, pick it up with the fork and enjoy. If the shrimp is bigger than one bite's worth, then spear it with your fork and cut it on the plate on which it's served. When faced with shrimp cocktail and no fork, simply hold the shrimp by the tail, dip it into the sauce, and take a bite. Fork or no fork, when the shrimp is big and the sauce is yours alone, you are free to double dip. If the sauce is communal, no double dipping.

Use the little oyster fork to get the clam or oyster to your mouth.

Soup

Dip the spoon into the soup to get a spoonful with a motion that takes the spoon away from you rather than toward you. You can gently rub the bottom of the spoon on the edge of the cup or bowl to catch any drip. It is acceptable to tip the bowl, too, but only for the last drop or two. Again, tip the bowl away from you, not toward you.

If oyster crackers come with the soup, place them on the underplate (the plate the bowl is sitting on) and add a few at a time to your soup; using your fingers for this is fine. Larger crackers, however, should stay out of the soup; eat them with your fingers instead of crumbling them into the bowl.

If the soup is served in a cup, it will come on a saucer. When you're done, place the spoon on the saucer. If the soup is served in a shallow bowl, place the spoon in the bowl with the handle positioned at four o'clock (pointing to the lower right). This position lets the waiter know you're finished with the soup.

Sorbet

This icy confection is served between the fish and meat courses; its purpose is to clear the palate. If the sorbet is served with a garnish, you may eat the mint leaves, fresh herbs, or flower petals.

Coffee

If your coffee cup is already on the table, it will be on your right, which is the same side all the other glasses go on.

Beverages

When wine is served, wait until your host has lifted his or her glass before you drink. Wait to sip beverages until your mouth is empty and has been wiped with a napkin. The only exception to this is when your mouth has been burned with hot food— when you may take a drink with food in your mouth. Do not gulp or guzzle beverages.

If you're asked by the hostess to pour the wine, fill the glass only one-third to halfway. If it's white wine, it will get warm if you fill it too high, and even if it's red, many people swirl their wine to enjoy the bouquet (aroma) of the wine. Swirling is considered an art, and it cannot be done properly if the glass is too full.

If you don't want wine, just place your fingertips lightly on the rim of the glass when the server approaches. Never turn the glass upside down. You should say something like "I'm not having any tonight." This lets others know that you do not necessarily disapprove of wine, and the others should feel free to enjoy their wine. Wine is served throughout the dinner.

Before you take a drink of water, wipe your lips with your napkin to remove excess lipstick or crumbs. Neither one would be very attractive on the edge of a water glass.

IV. SOME GENERAL TABLE MANNERS

1. Dealing with Food

Seasonings and Condiments

Guests should always taste the food before asking for salt and pepper, so as not to offend the cook. When you use the condiments on the table, place a portion of each condiment desired on the plate beside the food, not directly on the food itself, i.e., cranberry sauce is placed on the dinner plate, not on the meat. If there are no condiments on the table, it is not polite to ask for them.

Reaching

Guests may reach for food that is close to them, as long as they do not have to stretch for it and do not reach across another guest. If the food is across the table, ask politely for it to be passed.

Removing food from mouth

If a piece of food must be removed from the mouth, do it the same way that it was put in and place it on the plate. That simply means if a piece of watermelon went in your mouth on a fork, the watermelon seeds come out on your fork. If something goes in your mouth with your fingers, like a fresh cherry, then the pit comes out in your hand. If you are uncomfortable using your fork to take something out of your mouth, you may remove something with your thumb and forefinger into a cupped hand. Then set it on the edge of your plate. A pit or small bone should be removed with fingers. The most important thing to remember when removing food is to do it with as little show as possible. If you need to remove something that has become lodged between your teeth, wait until you're alone to do so.

Dealing with disagreeable food

When food that you don't like or can't eat is served, rather than make an issue and offend the hostess, take a small portion. Place the portion on the plate, dabble with it, and eat a small amount (or none at all). To compensate, take larger portions of other foods. For a severe allergy, say, "No, thank you" and after the meal, quietly explain to the hostess. At a buffet, take only the foods you like. If your hostess wants to serve you but you don't want to eat it, say, "Thank you. It looks very good, but I'm not quite used to American food yet. Maybe next time, thanks.

What do you say or do if you've accidentally taken too much food and you cannot possibly eat it all?

Say:

"I'm sorry, but it seems that 'my eyes are bigger than my stomach'."

Or

"I'm sorry. It was so delicious but I am full."

The main thing is not to offend your host.

Removing different foods from a platter at one time

When a platter contains a combination of foods, such as meat, potatoes, vegetable, and garnish, take a moderate serving of each, including the garnish. However, if the removal of garnish will overly disturb the appearance of the platter, leave it. If a course is presented with another food underneath, such as toast or lettuce, take the entire portion.

How large a portion to take from a platter

When a platter of pre-sliced food is presented, and each slice is an ample size, take one serving. But if the slices are small, and it looks as if there are enough servings for each guest to have two, take two for yourself. As a courtesy to the last guest, make sure to leave enough food on the platter so he or she has a choice from several portions.

Which portion to take from a platter

Rather than rummage through a platter and disturb the look of the presentation, take the portion nearest to you.

2. Conversation

Years ago at a formal affair, it was customary for the hostess to begin conversation at the table with the guest seated on her right. The guests followed suit, and in this way, no one was omitted from conversation. Halfway through the meal, the hostess directed her conversation to the guest seated on her left, and the guests did the same, a custom known as *turning the table*. Today the dinner table is no longer deliberately "turned," and a courteous guest makes sure he or she talks with the partners on both right and left sides.

How many people does one converse with at the table?

A formal table is laid with several candelabra and multiple tall centerpieces that block cross-table visibility and make conversation with those seated on the opposite side difficult. For ease of conversation at a formal affair, guests converse with their dinner partners and chat only briefly with those seated several places away (so the person in the middle does not have to lean backward). Do not yell to the ends of the table. You should speak in low tones but you do not have to act like you are in Church or a Public Library—dinner is meant to be enjoyed and the conversation is a fundamental part of that. But at an informal meal, because fewer courses are served and the table setting is simpler, cross-table visibility is not blocked and group conversation is encouraged.

Party Conversation

Party conversation should be light, non-threatening and definitely fun. Give the person you're speaking to your undivided attention. Also, keep a mental check that you aren't talking too much yourself. You should give equal time to the person sitting on your left and your right. It can be difficult to talk easily with strangers but it is absolutely imperative that you do so that everyone can join in on the conversation.

Unless you know every guest at the table very well, you should not discuss politics, religion, money, or sex at the table. You should also avoid any controversial subjects that may fall outside of the scope of those four topics. Those are very interesting subjects, but they're also emotional. Dinner is meant to be enjoyed, not to be a forum for debate.

You may say, "Tell me about yourself." But don't ask "What do you do?" If you'd like to know how they're employed, and they didn't offer, you may ask, "What is your profession?" It may be considered impolite however, since not everyone is employed. If they told you anything about themselves when you asked, they probably would have mentioned employment.

It is impolite to correct other people at anything, whether it be table manners, speech, or golf. Some people may appreciate a worthwhile comment, but be careful. The only time you should do so is when you are alone, you know the person very well, and you deliver the message with the utmost kindness.

When talking at the table, there should never be any food in your mouth. Remember the saying, "Don't talk with your mouth full! " Chew with your mouth closed, without talking. Guests should not draw attention to themselves by making unnecessary noise either with their mouth or with their silverware.

Thanks for service

Each time service is provided at a multi-course meal, verbal acceptance is not necessary because it distracts from the conversation. Acceptance of the course is in itself thanks. But to refuse service, a verbal rejection of "No, thank you," is given. At a simple meal when a serving bowl is passed upon request, it is courteous for the receiver to say, "Thank you." It is not necessary for those who receive a dish in passage to say thank you.

3. If You Take a Break or Leave the Table during the Meal

Place the napkin on your chair. If the server does not push the chair back under the table, you should do so. The server may also refold your napkin and place it on the arm of your chair during your absence.

When eating in formal situations, rest the fork and knife on the plate between mouthfuls, when you want to pause during a course, or for a break for any reasons. The knife and fork are crossed on the plate, with the fork over the knife and the tines pointing down. The knife should be in the 10:20 position, and fork (tines down and over the knife) should be at the 2:40 position.

Resting positions

4. Smoking at the Table

A lighted cigarette is never taken to the table. Smoking is offensive to nonsmokers and dulls the palate. A table laid without ashtrays indicates that the hostess does not wish her guests to smoke. But if ashtrays are provided, before proceeding to smoke and as a courtesy to others, ask the hostess for permission. Because some people are allergic to smoke, wait until the table is cleared for dessert or hold off until dessert is finished. Never use a dessert plate or a saucer as an ashtray.

5. I Dropped My Fork!

Traditionally, if you dropped a piece of silverware, you were to leave it where it fell and simply tell a server, so he or she can bring you another. Today if you drop a piece of your silverware, and it is easily within reach, it's all right to pick it up. Give it to the serving person, and ask for another. If it is out of your reach, under the table, or someone else's chair, simply tell the server, and they will bring you another. (Don't use silverware that has fallen on the floor.)

If a little bit of food gets on the table, you may pick it up with the edge of your knife, and place it on the edge of your plate.

6. Spilled Food

When a guest spills food at a formal affair, a butler takes the appropriate action. But at an informal meal, the diner quietly and quickly lifts the food with a utensil and places it on the side of his plate. However, if food is spilled on another guest, the diner apologizes and offers to pay for cleaning (but let the other person wipe up the debris).

If a server has spilled something, they attend to it. If it is something a guest has spilled, and it is quite a mess, the guest simply apologizes, and allows it to be cleaned up.

7. I'm finished

Try to finish each course at about the same time as others around you. When you are finished with a course, you should indicate that. Here's how: Visualize a clock face on your plate. Place both the knife and fork in about the 10:20 position with the points at 10 and the handles at 20. The tines of the fork should be down or up and the blade of the knife should face you. Never put a dirty piece of silverware on the tablecloth. Don't push your plate away when you're finished eating. Simply leave it where it is. Someone will come and take it soon enough. Also, don't announce, "Boy am I stuffed," or "I couldn't eat another bite if I had to." Anything like that is considered rude. It is appropriate to say, "What a lovely meal this has been!" or something similar.

For more formal dinners, from course to course, your tableware will be taken away and replaced as needed. To signal that your are done with the course, rest your fork, tines up, and knife blade in.

At the end of the meal, do not refold the napkin. Pick it up from its center and place it loosely on the table to the left of your plate.

Toothpicks are not usually on the table in a home. **After the meal,** go to the bathroom and clean your teeth if you need to. In restaurants, they are usually at the counter where you pay as you go out. Again, it is

best to clean your teeth in the bathroom.

V. TOASTING AND TOASTS

1. Toasting

Toasting can make even a meal at the local diner a special occasion. It can add a festive air to a gathering and has a way of bringing everyone at the table together.

Who proposes a toast?

- The host proposes a toast first.
- If the host has stage fright, it is acceptable to have his or her spouse make the toast.
- The guest of honor or any guest who has been toasted should toast the host in return.
- In other cases, a guest may also propose a toast, but only after the host.

When to toast and for what?

- The host often proposes a toast at the beginning of the meal, welcoming a guest to it.
- The toast may also occur in the middle of the meal, when the host raises a glass to the guest of honor on his or her right.
- Instead of offering the toast at the beginning, the host might want to wait until the end. In that case, he or she would stand and toast the guest of honor.

2. Toasts

It has been said that toasts are like a woman's skirt. They should be long enough to cover the subject, but short enough to be amusing. That usually translates into about one minute.

An example of an excellent toast was given at a dinner for Nobel Prize winners in the State Dining Room of the White House. President John F. Kennedy rose and said, "I think this is the most extraordinary collection of talent, of human knowledge, ever gathered at the White House, with the possible exception of when Thomas Jefferson dined here alone."

You don't have to be that clever. A typical welcoming toast might be "I am so pleased that you all could be here to share each other's good company and this good food. Welcome." (at the beginning of the meal)

Or

"I am so pleased that you could all be here to welcome my dear friend Florence, who's come all the way from Rome to visit." (in the middle)

Or

"It's wonderful to have Florence with us tonight. Let's toast a rare woman who looks at every situation in life as an opportunity to give of herself, to make things better, happier, and more fun. To Florence." (at the end)

3. Beverage Choice

Toasting traditionally involves alcoholic beverages. Champagne (or at least some variety of sparkling wine) is regarded as especially festive and is widely associated with New Year's Eve and situations of a sudden, congratulatory nature (such as learning that one has gained a lucrative business contract).

There is no requirement that beverages contain alcohol, but it isn't uncommon for a person who is not drinking alcohol on a given occasion to take just a sip of an alcoholic beverage in honor of the toast in preference to a soft drink.

Often, different participants have different drinks, such as when some people drink sparkling cider instead of sparkling wine.

4. Dos and Don'ts

A wonderful toasting makes gathered guests feel honored to be together and with you, whereas a bad one just embarrasses everyone. Here are some **dos** and **don'ts** to help you shine.

Dos

✔ Do make a toast even if you are not drinking alcohol. Anything will do. It is the thought that counts.

✔ Do toast the host in return if you are the guest of honor and are being toasted. You can do this as soon as the host's toast is finished or later, during dessert. Just keep it short.

✔ Do toast more than one person. For example, you might toast an entire family that has come to visit, or a whole team.

✔ Do keep your toast short.

Don'ts

✖ Do not ever toast yourself.

✖ Do not preempt. The host should be the first one to toast.

✖ Do not read your toast. If it is too long to commit to memory, it is too long. Come up with something pithier.

✖ Do not clink glasses. It is an old custom involving the driving away of spirits— not a happy thought at any occasion. Besides, it is bad news for glassware.

✖ Do not tap the rim of your glass to get everybody's attention—it is tacky.

In western culture, if you are the one being toasted, just listen quietly to the toast and then say a quick thank-you. Do not even put your hand on your glass, much less drink. Or people joining in the toast may signify their agreement by lifting their drinks into the air, often accompanied by shouted or murmured sounds of agreement, either repeating the toast word (e.g., "Cheers!") or confirming the sentiment with terms such as "Hear! Hear!", and often followed by touching one's drinkware against those of everyone else within reach.

However, certain cultures outside that sphere have their own traditions in which consuming a drink is connected with ideas of celebration and honor.

For example, a toast to others is a characteristic of Chinese dining, too. When all people are seated and all cups are filled, the host should toast others first, together with some simple prologue to let the dining start. During the dining after the senior's toast, you can toast anyone from superior to inferior at their convenience. When someone toasts you, you should immediately stop eating and drinking to accept and toast in response. If you are far from someone you want to toast, then you can use your cup or glass to rap on the table to attract attention rather than raise your voice. However, it is impolite to urge others to drink.

Section Five   When the Dinner Is Over

Does inviting someone to a business lunch, dinner, or breakfast mean they are obligated to reciprocate? Not necessarily. The rules governing the reciprocation of invitations vary from situation to situation.

You are not expected to repay an invitation to a strictly-business meal (especially one charged to an expense account), no matter who invited you—a customer, a client, or your boss. But you may certainly do so if you have continuing business together.

A client who is entertained by a salesperson or supplier is not expected to return the invitation, even if his or her spouse or family was invited.

Do return social invitations from coworkers and other business associates, whether they've extended the hand of friendship to cement a business relationship or you simply enjoy one another's company away from the office. You needn't reciprocate in kind. For example, you could have your associate join you for a cookout as your thank-you for a restaurant dinner.

Practice   You Are an Expert!

I. Etiquette and Culture

1. First read the following short story written by Maugham; then try to answer the questions for discussion after the story, with the help of what you have learned in this unit.

The Luncheon

I caught sight of her at the play and in answer to her beckoning I went over during the interval and sat down beside her. It was long since I had last seen her and if someone had not mentioned her name, I hardly think I would have recognized her. She addressed me brightly.

"Well, it's many years since we first met. How time does fly! We're none of us getting any younger. Do you remember the first time I saw you? You asked me to luncheon?"

Did I remember?

It was twenty years ago and I was living in Paris. I had a tiny apartment in the Latin Quarter overlooking a cemetery (公墓) and I was earning barely enough money to keep body and soul together. She had read a book of mine and had written to me about it. I answered, thanking her, and presently I received from her another letter saying that she was passing through Paris and would like to have a chat with me; but her time was limited and the only free moment she had was on the following Thursday; she was spending the morning at the Luxembourg and would I give her a little luncheon at Foyot's afterwards? Foyot's is a restaurant at which the French senators eat and it was so far beyond my means that I had never even thought of going there. But I was flattered and I was too young to have learned to say no to a woman. (Few men, I may add, learn this until they are too old to make it of any consequence to a woman what they say.) I had eighty francs (gold francs) to last me the rest of the month and a modest luncheon should not cost more than fifteen. If I cut out coffee for the next two weeks I could manage well enough.

I answered that I would meet her at Foyot's on Thursday at half past twelve. She was not so young as I expected and in appearance imposing rather than attractive. She was in fact a woman of forty (a charming age, but not one that excites a sudden and devastating passion at first sight), and she gave me the impression of having more teeth, white and large and even, than were necessary for any practical purpose. She was talkative, but since she seemed inclined to talk about me I was prepared to be an attentive listener.

I was startled when the bill of fare was brought, for the prices were a great deal higher than I had anticipated (预计). But she reassured (保证) me. "I never eat anything for luncheon," she said. "Oh, don't say that!" I answered generously.

"I never eat more than one thing. I think people eat far too much nowadays. A little fish, perhaps. I wonder if they have any salmon (鲑鱼)." Well, it was early in the year for salmon and it was not on the bill of fare, but I asked the waiter if there was any. Yes, a beautiful salmon had just come in—it was the first they had had. I ordered it for my guest. The waiter asked her if she would have something while it was being cooked.

"No," she answered, "I never eat more than one thing. Unless you had a little caviar (鱼子酱). I never mind caviar." My heart sank a little. I knew I could not afford caviar, but I could not very well tell her that. I told the waiter by all means to bring caviar. For myself I chose the cheapest dish on the menu and that was a mutton chop. "I think you're unwise to eat meat," she said. "I don't know you can expect to work after eating heavy things like chops. I don't believe in overloading (超负荷) my stomach."

Then came the question of drink. "I never drink anything for luncheon," she said. "Neither do I," I answered promptly. "Except white wine," she proceeded as though I had not spoken. "These French white wines are so light. They're wonderful for the digestion." "What would you like?" I asked, hospitable (好客的) still, but not exactly effusive (热情的). She gave me a bright and amicable (和蔼的) flash of her white teeth. "My doctor won't let me drink anything but champagne."

I fancy I turned a trifle pale. I ordered half a bottle. I mentioned casually that my doctor had absolutely forbidden me to drink champagne. "What are you going to drink, then?" "Water." She ate the caviar and she ate the salmon. She talked gaily of art and literature and music. But I wondered what the bill would come to. When my mutton chop arrived she took me quite seriously to task.

"I see that you're in the habit of eating a heavy luncheon. I'm sure it's a mistake. Why don't you follow my example and just eat one thing? I'm sure you'll feel ever so much better for it." "I am only going to eat one thing," I said, as the waiter came again with the bill of fare. She waved him aside with an airy gesture.

"No, no, I never eat anything for luncheon. Just a bite, never want more than that, and I eat that more as an excuse for conversation than anything else. I couldn't possibly eat anything more—unless they had some of those giant asparagus (芦笋). I should be sorry to leave Paris without having some of them." "Madame wants to know if you have any of those giant asparagus," I asked the waiter.

I tried with all my might to will him to say no. A happy smile spread over his broad, priest-like face, and he assured me that they had some so large, so splendid, so tender, that it was a marvel. "I'm not in the least hungry," my guest sighed, "but if you insist I don't mind having some asparagus." I ordered them. "Aren't you going to have any?" "No, I never eat asparagus." "I know there are people who don't like them. The fact is, you ruin your palate (味觉) by all the meat you eat."

We waited for the asparagus to be cooked. Panic (惊慌) seized me. It was not a question now of how much money I should have left over for the rest of the month, but whether I had enough to pay the bill. It would be mortifying (耻辱的) to find myself ten francs short and be obliged (被迫) to borrow from my guest. I could not bring myself to do that.　I knew exactly how much I had and if the bill came to more I had made up my mind that I would put my hand in my pocket and with a dramatic（戏剧性的）cry start up and say it had been picked.　Of course it would be awkward if she had not money enough either to pay the bill.　Then the only thing would be to leave my watch and say I would come back and pay later.

The asparagus appeared.　They were enormous, succulent（多汁的）, and appetizing. The smell of the melted butter tickled my nostrils as the nostrils of Jehovah were tickled by the burned offerings of the virtuous Semites. I watched the abandoned woman thrust them down her throat in large voluptuous（奢侈无度的）mouthfuls and in my polite way I discoursed（谈论）on the condition of the drama in the Balkans. At last, she finished.

"Coffee?" I said. "Yes, just an ice cream and coffee," she answered. I was past caring now,　so I ordered coffee for myself and an ice cream and coffee for her. "You know, there's one thing I thoroughly believe in," she said, as she ate the ice cream. "One should always get up from a meal feeling one could eat a little more." "Are you still hungry?" I asked faintly. "Oh, no. I'm not hungry; you see, I don't eat luncheon. I have a cup of coffee in the morning and then dinner, but I never eat more than one thing for luncheon. I was speaking for you." "Oh, I see!"

Then a terrible thing happened.　While we were waiting for the coffee,　the head waiter, with an ingratiating（讨好的）smile on his false face, came up to us bearing a large basket full of peaches. They had the blush of an innocent girl; they had the rich tone of an Italian landscape. But surely peaches were not in season then? Lord knew what they cost. I knew too—a little later, for my guest, going on with her conversation, absentmindedly took one.

"You see, you've filled your stomach with a lot of meat—my one miserable little chop—and you can't eat any more.　But I've just had a snack and I shall enjoy a peach." The bill came and when I paid it I found that I had only enough for a quite inadequate tip. Her eyes rested for an instant on the three francs I left for the waiter and I knew that she thought me mean.　But when I walked out of the restaurant I had the whole month before me and not a penny in my pocket. "Follow my example," she said as we shook hands, "and never eat more than one thing for luncheon." "I'll do better than that," I retorted. "I'll eat nothing for dinner tonight." "Humorist!" she cried gaily, jumping into a cab. "You're quite a humorist!"

But I have had my revenge（复仇）at last.　I do not believe that I am a vindictive man, but when the immortal gods take a hand in the matter it is pardonable to observe the result with complacency（自鸣得意）. Today she weighs twenty-one stone.

Questions:

1. What dishes did the woman order? What kinds of courses did they belong to?

2. In your opinion, was the woman's order fancy or simple? Why?

3. If in the business world, do you think what the woman had done is appropriate or not? Give your reasons.

4. If you were the waiter, what would you think of the tip that "I" gave? Why?

2. Make a comparison between western and Chinese table manners after reading the following passage about Chinese table manners.

Chinese Table Manners

Seat arrangement

Chinese diet has a long history. In the country which has been a nation of etiquette and particular about food being the first necessity of the people since antiquity, dining etiquette has naturally become an important part of dining culture.

The banquet etiquette of China is said to originate from Lord Zhou. Through thousands of years of evolution, it has finally developed a set of universally accepted dining etiquette up to the present. It is the inheriting and developing of the dining ritual system in ancient times.

Dining etiquette varies with the character and purpose of a banquet and in different areas; it also differs in a thousand ways. The dining etiquette in ancient times is divided according to social strata: palace, local authorities, trade associations and folk society, etc. Whereas, modern dining etiquette is simplified as: master and guests.

As a guest, people should be particular about appearance when attending a banquet and determine whether to bring small gifts or good wine along according to the degree of relationship. They should also keep the appointment and be punctual. After they arrive, they should first introduce themselves or let the master do the introduction if unknown to others, and then comply with the master's arrangement and take the seat. The seating arrangement is the most important part in the whole Chinese dining etiquette.

From ancient times to the present, owing to the evolution of dining furniture, the arrangement of seats has been changing accordingly. On the whole, the order of seats is: taking the seats on the left and facing the east or the entrance gate as the seat of honor. The seat of honor in a family banquet is reserved for the elder with the highest position in the family hierarchy and the least prominent seat for the one with the lowest position.

When a family holds a banquet, the seat of honor is for the guest with the highest status and the master takes the least prominent seat. If the guest of honor is not seated, other people are not allowed to be seated. If he hasn't eaten, others should not begin to eat.

When making the rounds of drinks, people drink a toast from the seat of honor down in order.

If it is a round table, then the one facing the entrance door is the guest of honor. The seats on the left hand are in turn second, fourth and sixth, etc, while those on the right hand are in turn third, fifth and seventh, etc, until they join together.

If it is an Eight Immortals table and there is a seat facing the entrance door, then the right seat facing the entrance door is for the guest of honor. If there is no seat facing the entrance door, then the right seat facing the east is the seat of honor. Then the seats on the left side of the seat of honor are the second, fourth, sixth and eighth and those on the right side are the third, the fifth and the seventh.

If it is a grand banquet, the arrangement of tables should be the table of honor placed in the front middle. The tables on the left are in turn the second, the fourth and the sixth and those on the right are the third, the fifth and the seventh. People take seat according to the identity, status and degree of relationship.

Dining Etiquette

When taking a dinner, people should behave in a civilized manner, pay attention to their own table manners and keep a good dining habit. Generally they should pay attention to the following several aspects:

Let the elders eat first or when you hear an elder say "let's eat", you start to eat.

When taking the dinner, you should hold the bowl with the thumb on the mouth of the bowl, the first finger, the middle finger and the third finger on the bottom and the palm of the hand empty. If you don't hold the bowl but bend over the table and eat facing the bowl, it will be regarded as bad table manners. Moreover, it will have the consequence of pressing the stomach and affecting digestion.

When helping yourself to the dishes, you should take food first from the plate nearby or facing you other than that in the middle or on the side of others. It's bad manners to use the chopsticks to burrow through the dishes in the plate and "dig for treasure" and keep your eyes glued to the plates. It is not appropriate to take too much food at a time. When finding some favorite dishes, you should not gobble them like whirlwind scattering wisps of cloud, nor put the plate in front of yourself and eat like a horse without further ado. You should consider your parents and siblings at the same table. If there is not much left in the plate and you want to "clean" it up, you should consult others. If they say they don't want it any more, then you can eat it up.

You should close your mouth to chew food well before you swallow it, which is not only better for digestion, but also the requirement of etiquette on the dinner table. You should by no means open your mouth wide, fill it with large pieces of food and eat up greedily, nor stretch your neck, open your mouth wide, extend your tongue to catch the food when carrying food. Don't put too much food into your mouth at a time. Otherwise, you will leave an avaricious impression on others.

You should behave elegantly when taking a dinner. When taking food, don't bump against your neighbor, nor splash the soup or let the soup drop onto the table. If the corner of your mouth is stained with rice, use a tissue or a napkin to wipe it off gently instead of licking it with your tongue. When chewing food, don't make noises. You had better not talk with others with your mouth full. Be temperate in telling a joke lest you might spew your food or the food might enter the windpipe and cause danger. If you really need to take with your families, you should speak small.

When spitting out bones, fish bones and dish dregs, use chopsticks or hand to take them and put them on the table in front of you instead of spitting them directly onto the table or the ground. If you want to cough or sneeze, use your hand or a handkerchief to cover your mouth and turn your head backwards. If you find sand in your mouth when chewing or phlegm in the throat, you should leave the dinner table and spit it out.

During the dinner, you should try to refill the bowl with rice yourself and take initiative to refill the bowl with rice and dishes for the elders. When the elders do that for you, you should express your thanks.

Be concentrated when taking the dinner. Some children watch TV or read papers when having their meals. It is a bad habit. It is not sanitary, and will influence the digestion and assimilation of food and do harm to eyesight.

In comparison, their
    similarities are:
    differences are:

II. Solve the Mystery: Why Was the Host Embarrassed?

In 1930 a Chinese official visited America. An American friend invited him to have a western dinner. After he sat down at the table, he used the napkin to clean the knives and forks. The host was so embarrassed that he asked the waiter to take away all the tableware on the table and bring other pairs.

III. Case Study

Imagine you are going to prepare a dinner for 12 people including the host, the hostess, the guest of honor and his wife, an unmarried man, an unmarried woman and other 3 married couples; draw respective diagrams to show your seat arrangement for a round table and a long rectangular table. Please make a point of the respective seats of the host, the hostess, the guest of honor and his wife, the unmarried man and the unmarried woman.

IV. Polite or Impolite

Which of the following behaviors are polite or impolite at a formal dinner? Write "P" (polite) or "I" (impolite) in brackets.

(   ) 1. Put your napkin on your lap.

(   ) 2. Start eating as soon as your food is served in front of you.

(   ) 3. Use your fingers when eating chicken.

(   ) 4. Finish eating everything on your plate.

(   ) 5. Talk loudly while eating.

(   ) 6. Make other people drink more spirits than they can take.

V. Form Filling

Decode the formal place setting below and fill out the form that follows.

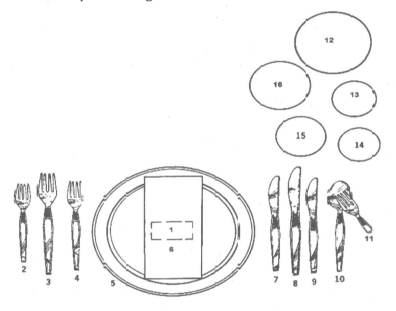

1.	2.	3.	4.	5.	6.
7.	8.	9.	10.	11.	12.
13.	14.	15.	16.	17.	18.

Another piece of advice:

Natural table manners take practice, and the best place to practice is at home. If manners at the table are insisted upon at home, they will more likely become second nature. Once good table manners become automatic you will feel more relaxed and comfortable, and the conversation and food will be enjoyed much more.

Chapter VI

Interview

First, please read the following excerpt from a speech of Harvey Mackay, best selling author and president of Mackay Envelope Corp., which is a true story of a young man who came to interview for a job at his company.

I asked him right off the bat what he had done to prepare for the interview. He said he had read something about us somewhere and that was about it.

Had he called anyone at Mackay Envelope Corporation to find out more about us? No. Had he called anyone who did business with our company? Our suppliers? Our customers? No.

Had he checked his university's alumni office to see if there were any graduates working at Mackay he could interview to learn about our corporate culture? Had he asked any students or teachers for their advice? To grill him in a mock interview? To share information? Did he contact the chamber of commerce, go to the library, locate some newspaper clippings on us, or check us out in D & B? If we'd been a publicly held company, which we aren't, could he have gotten his hands on our annual report and any brokerage house recommendations?

Did he write us a letter before he came in to tell us about himself, what he's doing to prepare for the interview and why he'd be right for the job? Was that letter a custom-made piece, for us and us only, not an all-purpose flyer? Did it show us his communication skills, his knowledge of our company, his eagerness to join us, and what he had to offer?

Was he planning to follow up after the interview, write us another letter indicating his continued high level of interest in the job? Had he planned a way to make sure the letter would be in our hands within twenty-four hours of the meeting, possibly even hand delivered?

The answer to every question was the same: no. That left me with only one other question: How well prepared would this person be if he were to call on a prospective customer for us? I already knew the answer.

> *Now please try to answer the following questions.*
>
> 1. Do you think this young man would be offered a position at the company? Why or why not?
>
> 2. Have you found any clue to interview etiquette? Share what you have found with your classmates.

Section One   Before the Interview

An interview might just last for 15 minutes, but all the work that you are supposed to do for the success of the interview would cost you days, weeks, even months. And most of the time you spend on the interview will be spent in preparing for it. You may ask: do I have to do that much homework before hand? Surely you do!

I. THE RESEARCH

1. Make Your Objective Clear to Yourself

This is simple. It is mostly about what you can do, what you want to do, what you want to get from your career and your job, both spiritual and material, and so on. A clear objective can guide you to make up your mind and help you make a choice. Of course, to answer all the questions, first you can make general lists and gradually narrow them down. Once you fix on less than 10 aims, you can start the research.

2. Research of the Labor Market

From newspapers, TV and radio broadcasting, the internet and some governmental institutions, you can get the information and data about the fields in which jobs are challenging but rewarding, or are easy to get; and your choice depends on your objective.

3. Research of the Companies

As Harvey Mackay put it, to know about the companies you want to work at, you can call the companies, call anyone who did business with them, such as the suppliers and the customers, check your university's alumni office, go to the library, locate some newspaper clippings, etc.

II. THE PAPER WORK

After doing the research, you should spare no effort to get your paper work ready.

1. Be sure

that you have worked out perfect:

- application letter/cover letter and

• resume;

(Please check Chapter 9 for working out good application letters and resumes.) and that you have enough photocopies of your:

• application letter/cover letter,

• resume and

• certificates and certified transcripts.

2. Do send them out to the companies you want to apply to for a position.

3. Expect to have your references checked prior to getting an offer.

Plan ahead and compile a list of references and some letters of recommendations, so that you are prepared when the employer requests them.

III. THE MOCK INTERVIEW

The mock interview can be done after you send the application, either before or after you get the reply from the company, which formally informs you of an interview. And you can certainly have yourself grilled in again and again. Just find a friend or a family member who would not mind taking all the trouble to help you out—acting as your interviewer.

1. A collection of Frequently Asked Questions in all interviews will be necessary. Here are some:

Interview Questions

Work History

● Name of company, position title and description, date of employment

● What were your expectations for the job and to what extent were they met?

● What were your starting and final levels of compensation?

● What were your responsibilities?

● What major challenges and problems did you face? How did you handle them?

● Which was most/least rewarding?

● What was the biggest accomplishment/failure in this position?

● What was it like working for your supervisor? What were his strengths and shortcomings?

● Why are you leaving your job?

● Why were you fired?

About You

● Describe a typical work week

● How many hours do you normally work?

● How would you describe the pace at which you work?

● How do you handle stress and pressure?

● What motivates you?

- What do you find are the most difficult decisions to make?
- If the people who know you were asked why you should be hired, what would they say?
- Do you prefer to work independently or on a team?
- Give some examples of team work.
- What type of work environment do you prefer?
- Describe a difficult work situation/project and how you overcame it.
- How do you evaluate success?

The New Job and Company

- What interests you about this job?
- What applicable attributes/experience do you have?
- Why are you the best person for the job?
- What do you know about this company?
- Why do you want to work for this organization?
- What challenges are you looking for in a position?
- What can you contribute to this company?
- Are you willing to travel?
- Is there anything I haven't told you about the job or company that you would like to know?

The Future

- What are you looking for in your next job? What is important to you?
- What are your goals for the next five years/ten years?
- How do you plan to achieve those goals?
- What are your salary requirements - both short-term and long-term?

In addition to being ready to answer these standard questions, prepare for behavior based interviewing.

This is based on the premise that a candidate's past performance is the best predictor of future performance. You need to be prepared to provide detailed responses including specific examples of your work experiences. The best way to prepare is to think of examples where you have successfully used the skills you've acquired.

If you were fired from your job, you will need to be prepared with an answer as to why you were fired.

Take the time to itemize your skills, values and interests as well as your strengths and weaknesses. Emphasize what you can do to benefit the company rather than just what you are interested in.

2. Have questions of your own ready to ask.

The last question you may be asked is "What can I answer for you?" You aren't simply trying to get this job—you are also interviewing the employer to assess whether this company and the position are a good fit for you. So, prepare yourself some questions that you can expect the interviewers to answer.

Sample Interview Questions to Ask about the Job

- Which specific skills are necessary to succeed in this job?
- Would you please describe the ideal candidate for this job?
- How do my skills, experience and education differ from those of the ideal candidate?
- What are the day-to-day duties of this job?
- Do you have anything to add to the job description that XYZ advertised?
- Does this job have any special demands?
- How much travel does this job require?
- How many hours are in a typical workweek?
- What is a typical workday like in this position?
- How would you describe the working environment?
- Are there specific problems or challenges an employee would face in this position?
- If you hire me, which duties would you like for me to accomplish first?
- Which projects would you like for me to complete in the next six months?
- What are the long-term objectives of this job?
- Who would be my immediate supervisor and where does he or she fit into the organization?
- Would you please describe your management style?
- Who would be my direct reports and what are they like?
- What are my potential coworkers like and how many are there?
- How much autonomy would I have in making decisions?
- What would be my budget and spending authority and responsibilities?
- What level of input would I have in determining my objectives and deadlines?
- How many projects must an employee in this position multitask at once?
- Are there opportunities for pay raises and advancement in this position?
- Is this a new position or am I replacing someone?
- Why was this new position created?
- May I ask why the employee in this position is leaving or no longer fills it?
- May I seek success tips from the employee who was promoted out of this position?
- Has anyone ever performed poorly in this position? What did he or she do wrong?
- How do you measure an employee's performance and provide feedback?
- How does an employee know he or she is performing this job to expectations before annual merit reviews?

Sample Interview Questions to Ask about the Company

- How does XYZ Company acknowledge outstanding employee performance?

- What are this department's goals and how do they fit with XYZ Company's?
- How does this department fit in with XYZ Company's five-year plan?
- Is this department responsible for its own profit and loss?
- Does the department or XYZ Company face any major challenges?
- Do you foresee any significant changes in XYZ Company?
- What's XYZ's policy about employees advancing their education?
- Does XYZ offer employee training?
- How does XYZ promote and support professional growth?
- What's XYZ's policy for work-life balance?
- What's XYZ's policy for employee retention?
- What is XYZ's customer service policy?
- Has XYZ recently laid off employees and why was it necessary?
- How did XYZ handle notification, severance and outplacement services during the last layoff?
- Is XYZ planning or considering a layoff in the near future?
- Is XYZ profitable? How profitable?
- Does XYZ regularly report its market results and profitability to its employees?
- How does XYZ compare with its competitors?
- How well has XYZ historically weathered poor economic conditions?
- May I ask what you like and don't like about XYZ Company?
- Is there anything you'd change about XYZ if you could?
- How would you characterize XYZ Company?
- Would you please describe XYZ's strengths and weaknesses?
- Are there any misconceptions about XYZ Company of which I should be aware?
- Does upper management have an open-door policy?
- What can you tell me about the employees who work here?
- May I see an organizational chart?

Sample Interview Questions to Ask in Summary

- Is there anything else I should know?
- Is there anything else you'd like to know?
- Is there anything that would prevent you from offering this job to me?
- How do I compare with the other candidates you've interviewed so far?
- Do you have any feedback?
- Do you have any concerns? What can I do to alleviate them?
- When can I expect to hear from you again?
- May I follow up with you by phone or email in about a week?
- May I schedule another interview with you?
- What might we discuss in a follow-up interview?

- If you decide to extend an offer, when would you like for me to start?
- What's the next step?

3. Do not practice too late the night before the day of the interview.

Practice earlier and have a good sleep.

IV. GET TO KNOW ABOUT THE SPOT FOR THE INTERVIEW

It's probably the first time for you to go to the company and if you are not familiar with the exact location, the route and what transportation you can take, check them out beforehand. The point is that you can calculate the time you have to spend in getting there and know when to leave home for the interview and be punctual.

V. DRESS UP!

After learning all that is about business dress and grooming in *Chapter II*, you can have the confidence of dressing yourself appropriately. Please remember that interview is one of the most formal occasions in the business world and dress yourself formally.

Admittedly we always hear about Casual Fridays of a lot of companies or according to your research, the company you are going to for the interview has a corporate culture of rather casual style. You are not, however, one of the employees of the company yet, so choose to *err on the conservative side*—it is better to be overdressed than to be underdressed.

Section Two   During the Interview

Finally comes the big day! Having ground your sword for such a long time, you are surely eager to try its sharpness in the real interview.

I. PUNCTUALITY

First of all, to make good impressions on the interviewers, you should **be on time** for the interview, that is to say, to arrive at the company 5 to 10 minutes earlier. Do not arrive too early, like 30 minutes ahead of schedule. It is said that the effect of 30 minutes early for an interview is the same as that of 5 minutes late for it and being late for an interview for even 1 minute is definitely unacceptable. Business persons always have tight schedules and too early arrival for the interview might interrupt the interviewer's other work. That is probably why you are expected to come only several minutes early.

II. BE THE TRUEST AND THE NICEST YOU

First I would like to share a story with you: A lot of candidates applied for a position in a well-known kindergarten. Some of them had high diplomas and others had shining previous work experience. While all the candidates were gathered in a waiting room to wait for their turns to be interviewed, they had a heated talk about the care and education of babies and little children, both in theory and in practice. A moment later, a receptionist entered and told them that they would be showed around the kindergarten before their interview, so they swarmed out of the room and followed the receptionist. They were so eager for the sightseeing that none of them noticed the little girl crying on their way and they just went on their visit, none except a young lady who bent down and gently wiped the tears out of the little girl's face and comforted her. And I believe that you already know the end of the story: this young lady got the offer of the job.

What the story is telling us is that our task in an interview is not only to win the interviewers over, but we also win other people round over through our courtesy and good manners. In this sense, anyone you meet at the company could be your interviewer. So try to be nice to the receptionist, the secretary, the assistant, even your competitors. And if you smoke, while you are waiting for your turn to come, do not ever smoke in a non-smoking area. Even when you are in the area that smoking is allowed, ask for others' permission before you light up a cigarette.

III. GENERAL TIPS DURING THE INTERVIEW

- **Smile, immediately offer a firm handshake, introduce yourself, and say something** like, "I'm pleased to meet you." or "I've been looking forward to talking with you." Be sincere and avoid informal greetings you might use to say hello to your friends. Take the polite, conservative route.
- **Read the mood.** If the interviewer is formal, then you probably should be, too. If the interviewer is casual, then follow along while remaining courteous and professional. In either case, try to appear to be relaxed, but not too relaxed. It's not a good idea to put your feet up on the interviewer's desk!
- Wait to be told to take a seat or ask if you may, then say thank you. This shows good manners.
- If it's possible without making a commotion, scoot your chair a little closer to the interviewer's desk or take the chair closer to the desk, like you're ready to dive right in. This shows interest and confidence.
- However, don't invade the interviewer's personal space, a perimeter of about 90cm by U.S. standards.
- Sit with good posture. If you don't know what to do with your hands, keep them folded on your lap. This is another indication of good manners. Avoid crossing

your arms over your chest, as it subliminally demonstrates a closed mind to some.

- Even formally-trained interviewers are regular people like you, so they'll expect you to be a little nervous while sitting in the "hot seat." Still, try to avoid obvious signs like fidgeting.
- Maintain eye contact with the interviewer. Avoid staring or you might make the interviewer uncomfortable, but don't look away too often either.
- To some, failure to maintain a comfortable level of eye contact indicates that you are lying, reaching for answers or lacking confidence.
- Don't eat, drink, chew gum or smoke, or even ask if it's okay. But if the interviewer offers coffee or other beverages, it's okay to accept. It's probably better to say "no thanks" to snacks (unless you're at an interview meal), so you don't accidentally drop crumbs in your lap, be forced to talk with your mouth full, and all that other stuff your mom told you not to do with your food.

Section Three   After the Interview

Immediately send a thank-you letter to each of your interviewers. (To get their contact information, ask for business cards during interviews.) Sending thank-you letters is professional and courteous, and will help to make you stand out in the minds of your interviewers. Besides, many interviewers expect it, and it's a good idea to do what interviewers expect.

Be prepared to attend two or three interviews at the same company. If you're called back for another interview, it means that they're interested in you. But they're also narrowing the competition, so keep up the good work!

Be patient. It's not unusual for interviewers to take weeks to narrow the competition. But if you don't hear from them in about a week or 24 hours or so after they said you'd hear from them, it's okay to send follow-up letters. (Don't call without permission. Interviewers might consider it rude of applicants to interrupt their workday with unsolicited calls.)

Practice

Roleplay: Work in groups. Group members are divided into two parties, respectively playing the roles of the interviewers and the interviewees. Prepare some questions to ask each other and think about how to answer the questions of the other party. You could switch the roles after the first round of the practice.

Chapter VII

Workplace Etiquette

Good office etiquette is easily achieved by using common courtesy as a matter of course. The essence of good manners and etiquette is to be respectful and courteous at all times and with everybody.

Section One   The Executive at Ease with Staff, Peers and Superiors

It is advisable that the ambitious students who aim to become business executives in future careers pay special attention to the following suggestions given by Professor Yang Junfeng, especially those prospective young managers.

I. THE ROLE OF A MANAGER

1. General Responsibilities of a Manager

A manager has a much larger responsibility than just the quality of his or her work. The manager of people is responsible for the morale of the office.

A good manager shows the ways:

- in giving credit where it is due in defining those who need it;
- in encouraging staff when they are feeling down;
- and in showing by his/her own example how to treat people, including the support staff, from the ground up.

2. The Smart Work of a Successful Manager

Remember that a chain is always as strong as its weakest link. There is no team without cooperation all along the line. So a successful manager never loses sight of the importance of his team. He/She:

- gives full credits to whomever deserves it—and does it in front of the staff;
- always uses "we" instead of "I" when represent a section or division;
- vigorously defends any staff member who has been unjustly accused, lobbies for another chance for any staff member who has been justly accused;

- never thoughtlessly encroaches on another manager's territory;
- set an example for the staff in environmental behavior;
- runs meetings efficiently and never calls one unless it is absolutely necessary;
- is an excellent meeting participant: pays attention to the agenda, refrains from wasting time, but adheres to the chairman's request;
- knows how to motivate employees in work and in good cause;
- makes certain employees are in the best impossible environment, with the proper ventilation, lighting, seating, sound and desk efficiency;
- is a consummate personal note writer—to thank, encourage, console, inspire or apologize to someone;
- goes out of the way, creatively, to help a colleague or friend who is in trouble;
- always returns borrowed property promptly and in good condition;
- discourages any hurtful rumor and plays a defense role when it comes to gossip;
- dresses appropriately for any occasion to reflect well on the company;
- is socially astute: answers all invitations promptly and attends any function on time and properly dressed;
- does not boast about invitations that others in the office have not received, nor discuss the event after it has occurred;
- is a considerate host, always mindful of his/her guests' comfort;
- is a considerate guest who keeps his/her eyes open and who helps when it is needed;
- is generous, and known for picking up the check at a difficult moment, when it is not his/her turn, to avoid a scene in the restaurant;
- knows protocol, adheres by its rules and understands deference to people of senior rank;
- knows how to give a compliment to others and to receive one graciously;
- understands that the quickest road to social failure is to be socially over-aggressive (i.e. pushy);
- has excellent telephone, cellular phone, e-mail, pager, and fax manners;
- encourages employees to better their lives, to further educate themselves and strive to be qualified for a higher level job;
- motivates employees, by example and financial support, to support and enjoy their area's cultural offerings;
- shows compassion for employees and tries to help solve problems with an imaginative use of the programs offered by the company. Sometimes these services don't even exist—until a manager makes them happen;
- understands that when communicating, some people he/she manages have better skills in written explanations, while others do better with oral ones. It's only fair to ask them to do what they do best;

- gives the support staff a good forum in which to exchange ideas and to ventilate complaints;
- makes the support staff feel really important to the company;
- When an employee has made a mistake, criticizes that person in private, but makes certain the employee understands exactly what was wrong (This requires great communication skills on the part of the manager, and also human skills— to reassume the employee that he is still of great value to the company, that everyone believes in that employee and that he should continue to work creatively and take risks, not just work gingerly for fear of making an error); and
- Has a sense of humor, because next to kindness, it's the greatest asset of all.

3. Treat the Secretary Kindly and Respectfully

Without the secretary, the manager is powerless. They make arrangement for the manager. If the secretary is very efficient, in two or more years time you'll promote your secretary.

Keep your promise. Everybody has desire and ambition to move up. You should be sensitive to their desire and ambition.

The manager is a person with influence. Therefore,

- Help your secretary to achieve his/her goal. Keep your promise.
- If the secretary leaves the company, you should be sure he/she will not set out the secret of your company. When time comes, you should push his/her out. He/she will appreciate your push.
- Treat your secretary kindly. The secretary is only as good as the amount of respect she receives from the boss. Pay her the bonus.

Introduce the Secretary Formally and Professionally

The secretary to visitor should be introduced by the boss as "Ms. Johnson," not as "Debbie Sue." To introduce him/her by his/her family name is to give him/her—and his/her job—a sense of dignity, a special status. When people from the outside are in and around his senior manager's office, even though they use given names in private, the boss and secretary should refer to one another by their family names.

e.g.

— *"Ms. Johnson, will you please get Mr. Ashton on the telephone?"*

— *"Certainly, Mr. Brainard."*

This way creates a much better image of the office to outside visitors present than the following exchange:

— *"Debbie Sue, get Bennie on the phone."*

— *"Yeah sure, Jerry."*

4. Treat New Employees Fairly

A good manager judges new employees fairly, according to the value of the new employee to the company. He/She:

- shows the employee the ropes on joining the company or firm, assisting without patronizing;
- praises the new employee's good performances and criticizes the poor ones, giving fair and accurate feedback on job performance;
- honestly appraises what the new employee contributes to the team effort. Including the successes that make him/her look good, too; and
- shows regard for the new employee as a team member, includes him/her in all the division's or firm's activities, and metes out her major responsibility.

5. Treat the Staff Equally and Respectfully

The competent executive who treats everyone in the office with equal respect and consideration will succeed because everyone in that office will want that person to enjoy success, and will assist.

This means that when you walk into your office building you greet everyone who crosses your path, even if you don't feel like it. You may have indigestion, a bad cold, or had a fight with your spouse that morning, or your teenage son managed to wreck your car, so you had to come on a crowded bus. Others aren't interested in your troubles. They may also be in need of cheering up, but instead of replaying your troubles to them, help them with theirs by putting on a positive face.

It may sound syrupy, but it is true: smiles are immensely contagious. A sudden warm, enthusiastic smile tossed at someone can change the whole temperature in the room at that time. No matter what ranking you hold within the organization, remember to say "hello" to everyone and to start an epidemic of smiles as people start their workdays. This is a message yet to be understood by groups of well-educated, employed, young executives.

6. A Good Manager Makes Friends at Work

For many people, the office is the primary arena of social life. Employees often do not have the resources, or perhaps the time, to make friends in their communities. The place of work, where so many hours in a week are spent, should be looked upon as a rich resource for establishing friendships. (If you are single, it is smart not to look upon it as a rich resource for romance, because it probably won't be.)

Good personal relationships at work are keys to happy, productive executives and to high morale in the entire workplace. In cultivating friendships, remember the following:

- Be open and friendly to everyone, not just to those who are especially popular or who have an almost celebrity status. Don't play favorites, in other words, or be overly aggressive in courting someone's friendship. It's fine to invite someone to lunch. It's not fine to invite someone to lunch five days in a row.
- Let the friendship develop slowly.

- Scout around for someone in the office who shares your passion in life whether it's playing tennis or golf, watching foreign film, taking cooking lessons, or attending concerts. The person who shares your major extra-curricular interest is the most logical potential friend.

- Be sensitive to the other people's schedule, such as work deadlines. It's as annoying to your executive friend as it is to his boss if you interrupt him when he's hard at work, on a deadline.

- Don't expect to share in your new friend's social life, at least at first. A friendship must grow logically and easily in the office, before the other person will want you to share his or her out-of-the-office life. In fact, don't be upset if you never become part of someone's out-of-the-office life.

- Don't be resentful of your friends' friendships in the office. Jealousy is the quickest deterrent to a good social relationship.

- Be supportive of your friend when he or she has had a success, basket in the reflected glory of it; when he has had a major disappointment, stand ready to cheer him up, encourage him and make him feel good about the future.

- Lead a helping hand when it is really needed for a good friend. That might consist of any of the following:
  - Lend money if he has had a personal emergency.
  - Lend your car in the case of a breakdown of his.
  - Stick up for him when he is unfairly criticized whether by his peers or his boss.
  - Report a piece of information you have that will benefit him—even if it's a criticism he needs to hear.
  - Assist him when he is in the midst of an office crisis. For example: copying documents he needs for an emergency meeting when the supposed staff has gone home for the day.

- Be sensitive to your friend's family obligations if they exist. Don't feel neglected or spurned if you are not invited to join your new friend during family weekend activities.

- You are much better off if you have several best friends. Having only one puts you at a disadvantage, particularly if he or she disappoints you, has his or her own personal problems or moves away.

- Be discreet in the office about your friendship. It is distracting if you and your friends broadcast to your office environment your every joint activity.

- Don't abuse your friendships. This means that you are carefully not to ask too many favors of friends, and you never put them on the spot.

- Use your really good friends to improve yourself. Ask them to give you frank answers to tough questions. (Do I really have an overly loud voice? Did I ramble too much in my presentation of the new plan this morning—should I have been more concise? Will you come with me when I order a new suit tomorrow, so I don't make a big mistake?)

II. THE YOUNG MANAGER

1. When the Young Manager Come to a New Company

When you come to the company, you should greet everybody and shake hands with them and ask each person his name and job. You should read everybody's biography carefully, age, sex, name, birthday, height, photo, family, etc. The other will be really flattered if you say "oh, you're a mother of twins," when you shake hands. You should demonstrate why you have been chosen the new manager. You should talk about your background, experience, special knowledge in some special area. These things will tell people you need to be respected. You should. You should finish the meeting with the people showing how pleased you are to be working on this job, to be working with them, explain to the worker that it is important to cooperate as a team, make sure you let them understand that you admire the cooperation team, and give them the confidence that you will be successful.

2. A Young Executive Deals with the Personal Problems of His Employees

A good manager is like a good general in the field—he takes care of the troops. When it comes to the manager's attention that an employee is having a serious problem, he takes action.

For example, if an employee comes to you with a legitimate complaint about another employee's personal mannerisms, do what you can to help so that everyone has an easier time of it. Tact and diplomacy may be required here. Discuss the problem privately with the employee and encourage his input in the solution to the problem. Be sure to check on the employee's progress and congratulate him, as well as anyone who helped, when the problem is under control.

For instance, some one likes eating garlic. John in the mail room may come into work every morning, reeking with garlic and without clean clothes. Tell him that people have been complaining about his odor. Say something he's been doing that's praise-worthy before you say goodbye. "John, I heard the mail room expenses are down this month. That's the way to go. Good work! "

If Suzie likes interrupting the others when they have conversation, if she continues to interrupt when you are talking privately with her, try giving her some of her own medicine. Begin interrupting her constantly yourself, always with a smile on your face so she knows exactly what you are doing. Tell her she needs to know how it feels to others when she constantly interrupts them.

3. The Young Manager Copes with the Older Employee

Hostility and resentment are full of the office. The old employee may ignore your presence and show no respect to you. If she says: I'm here for 30 years, you're new.

What do you know?

When you face this, what would you say?

Say something like "Though I'm not experienced, I know how to hold you experienced people together. I'm here because I have found the company weak and with problem. Everybody here works together with me and makes it appropriate again."

Section Two Employee Etiquette

At this information age, it becomes apparent that the cubicle has become the standard business configuration, even for managers. For those of us not lucky enough to telecommute, the cube has become our home—albeit small—away from home.

I. BUILDING RELATIONSHIPS

1. You and Your Company—Respect

- Respect the business goals and help to achieve them.
- Respect the firm's confidentiality of information.
- Respect the firm's clients' confidentiality of information.

2. You and Your Employer

- Be respectful to your employer.
- Cooperate with your employer.
- Provide your boss with information as required.
- Keep your boss well informed in a timely fashion.
- If your boss criticizes your work, enquire about what precisely is wrong with it, consider the comments, discuss them amiably if you disagree with the comments but defer to the boss's opinion if he/she is adamant. The boss always gets the benefit of the doubt. Don't argue with the boss. (however, there are standards of etiquette for employers too.)

3. Watch Your Own Steps

- Wear proper attire.
- Be on time for your job. Better still, be early.
- NEVER arrive at work drunk, smelling of alcohol or under the influence of drugs.
- Keep your work area tidy. Try not to be messy.

- "Mute" your cell phone in the office. No fancy ring tones.
- Do not "big note" yourself, there is no place for arrogance in this world.
- Surveys show that the office know-it-all proved to be the biggest gripe amongst co-workers. Don't be a know-all.
- Practice good manners and office etiquette at every opportunity.

4. You and Your Co-Workers

- Respect all other employees and cooperate with all of them.
- Always be particularly respectful to those older than yourself even if they are junior to you in position. They are generally more mature in judgment and life's experiences and this deserves your respect even in the workplace.
- Show appreciation for the slightest courtesies extended to you.
- Show consideration for other people's feelings.
- Make new employees feel welcome and comfortable around you. Don't be a busy-body.
- Do not try to sell things to your colleagues.
- Avoid sexist comments about a co-worker's dress or appearance.
- If there is conflict, do not get personal in your remarks.

Offering and Receiving Criticism

Giving and receiving criticism is difficult. Unfortunately, it is a part of the corporate life. It should be directed to a person's work and professional conduct, nothing related to a persons personality or physical appearance.

Always criticize privately, politely, precisely, and promptly, while always take criticism professionally, politely, positively and properly.

If You Made a Mistake

Take responsibility for your mistakes, apologize and go about correcting it.

Apologize if you are clearly in the wrong. If in doubt, apologize anyway. It's no big deal.

Never blame someone else if it is your mistake.

II. RULES FOR CUBICLE ETIQUETTE

Although we now have voicemail and e-mail, it seems that some simply would rather holler. To this end, 22 rules are assembled for cubicle etiquette, which should help to promote greater thoughtfulness in today's office environment.

1. Eavesdrop Inconspicuously

Although you don't mean to eavesdrop, often you simply can't help it—the walls of cubicles rarely reach over 1.5 or 1.8 meters in height, so sound easily finds its way over the top. When someone adjacent to you asks someone a question for which you know the correct answer, resist the urge to volunteer this information. This action will only confirm that you were eavesdropping, even if it was unintentional.

2. Get an Invitation

- Show respect for each other's workspace. Knock before entering.
- Do not enter another cubicle unless you are invited.
- Do not stand outside a cube to conduct a conversation. Converse either in your cube or in that of your colleague.

3. Do Not Be a Pest

Do not use sign language or whisper to attract the attention of someone who is on the phone. You can return later to carry out a conversation if you see someone dialing, checking e-mail or voice mail, or involved in another activity.

4. Respect Meditation

Think twice before interrupting someone who appears to be deep in thought. They probably are. Keep your interruptions of others to a minimum and always apologize if your intrusion is an interruption of a discussion, someone's concentration or other activity.

5. Be a Soft Talker

Be aware of how your voice carries. Always use your "library voice" when speaking in a cubicle environment.

6. Do Not Play with Electronics

Avoid using your speakerphone for conversations and voicemail retrieval. Also, if you listen to compact discs in your CD drive or to Internet radio, use your headphones. There simply is no reason to subject others to your taste in tunes.

7. Keep Private Matters Private

Do not exchange confidential information in a cubicle. If you would not want it published in the local newspaper, do not discuss it in your cube. Try to find a meeting room, or take your conversation outside.

8. Suffer Alone

If you are ill, stay home. No one likes a martyr. Nor does anyone appreciate taking your cold or flu home to his or her loved ones. Understand that the first few days of an illness are the most dangerous in terms of contagion, and work from home during this time if possible.

9. Kick Others out Gracefully

Walk toward the entrance of your cubicle when you would like to keep an impromptu meeting short. You can stand up and say you need to go to the restroom or make a copy. Be creative.

10. Keep Snacking to a Minimum

The smell, noise, and mess of snack foods may be offensive to others. Also, some people are allergic to certain snacks such as peanuts, and popcorn can make others nauseous.

11. Decorate with Taste

Whether you furnish your office space with lava lamps and throw pillows or company policies and flow charts, remember that your cube is viewed by others throughout the day. Keep the half-nude pop icons and risqué cartoons to a minimum. Others may be offended on moral, religious, cultural, or sexual grounds. And who needs a complaint filed against them?

12. Prevent Distractions

If possible, arrange your desk to face away from your cubicle opening. Less eye contact could mean fewer interruptions.

Also, avoid eye contact with others walking by if you do not want to be interrupted.

13. Do Not Sneak up on Others

Not everyone has a cute rear-view mirror mounted on his or her monitor. And unless you can bring someone out of cardiac arrest with cardiopulmonary resuscitation or a defibrillator, follow the practice of knocking on a cube wall, saying "Excuse me," or otherwise letting your presence be known before launching a discourse.

14. Be Cautious with Foliage

Although serving as good noise buffers, plants tend to drop leaves and leak water—and not only in your cubicle. Don't overdo it; a conservative approach usually is better than cultivating a jungle. Remember that others may have allergies to certain plants, so you may want to discuss ornamental horticulture with your work mates before bringing in the landscapers.

15. Respect Privacy

When working in a shared space, suggest to the others that you take lunch breaks at different times to allow each of you some quiet time. Don't gossip about any co-worker's private life.

16. Avoid Eating Strong Foods at Your Desk

If possible, eat your Limburger cheese sandwich or roasted garlic and onion pizza in a cafeteria or break room.

17. Watch Your Micro Maize

Do not leave your snack unattended in a microwave. Little smells worse than burnt popcorn wafting through everyone's area.

18. Plan Construction Projects For After Hours

Rearrange your filing bins and reconfigure your shelving after most people have left for the day. Or do it on a weekend. Others may be trying to work during your renovation.

19. Get Some Exercise

Resist the urge to ask your cube neighbor a question "over the wall." Get up and stick your head around the corner, send an email or instant message, or call on the phone to ask if your colleagues are available. Besides disturbing them, you will be disturbing everyone else by blurting out your query or comment.

20. Plan for Day Care

Working parents should plan for appropriate childcare. No matter how cute your little angels are, your coworkers probably will not appreciate having a nursery next door.

21. Mind Your Business Elsewhere

Use a pay phone, other remote phone, or cell phone (outside the office) for private phone conversations. No one cares to listen to your wedding plans, confrontations with your spouse, or details of your latest hot date.

22. Do Not Offend the Olfactory

Scents travel as easily as sounds over cube walls. Use scented personal products in moderation.

A good rule of thumb for cubicle etiquette is that if it bothers you when others do it, avoid doing it yourself. Set a good example for colleagues. As the saying goes, "It is better to be a part of the solution than a part of the problem."

III. THE MANNERS AND IMPORTANCE OF THE SECRETARY

A secretary or administrative assistant with beautiful manners greatly enhances her/his organization. And she/he sets the tune for everyone in it. She/he elevates the entire corporate image by the tactful, considerate way in which she (or he) handles the relationships between the boss and the world inside and outside the company. A good secretary handles people so gracefully that when they've been told "no" they go away satisfied all the time.

However, the secretarial profession is one of the least appreciated and understood in the entire spectrum of jobs. The truth is that most of the true professionals in this field who have been with their companies for years know more than their bosses do about business. That fact is accepted by their appreciative, high-ranking managers, who admit that they do their jobs more brilliantly because the person behind the desk in the outer offices is doing that job brilliantly.

Chapter VIII

The Art of Making Phone Calls

Mr. X is calling Mr. Y, who lives upstairs.

Nobody answers the phone.

Mr. X sticks his head out of the window and shouts upward.

"Anybody up there?"

Mr. Y answers, "Yeah! What?"

" Answer the phone!"

At the new era of technology,   most people have telephones and mobile phones. We make more phone calls than we ever did in the last twenty years. This means of communication indicates a great opportunity for us to use our knowledge of business etiquette to make communicating easier and more pleasant for all the people concerned.

Voice and Attitude

The first thing to mention in phone etiquette is to pay attention to your tone of voice and your attitude.   People at the other side of the line may not see your face,   but they could sense your attitude because your tone of voice alone gives expression to the words spoken.

If you want to make your voice sound more pleasant,   you might try the following ways:

- Speak with a rising inflection. It will sound cheerful and friendly. Be careful not to overdo it and speak in a voice that is pitched high like that of the saleswomen in the shoe stores. That will be tiring, not only to you, but to the listener.

- Talk directly into the mouthpiece and speak with clarity. When someone has to ask you to repeat, bring the phone nearer and continue to speak clearly, but not more loudly.   The louder voice may convey the information to the listener that you are impatient to his request.

- Slow down if you are used to speaking rapidly. A pleasant voice that we'd like to hear is one that has no suggestion of hurry, annoyance or excitement. Although you don't mean to sound that you are in a hurry, it will seem as if you are anxious to cut the person off, and it will be very impolite.

- Cough or sneeze far away from the phone. Don't scare the listener with the noise you make while coughing or sneezing. It's common politeness to place our hands over the mouthpiece when we cough or sneeze because it shows your respect to the person. After that, "Excuse me" could be said to apologize for the interruption of the conversation.

- Try to speak politely. The way you should speak on the phone in a business setting is very different from the way you speak to your best friend. Being too direct and frank might make the person at the other side of the line feel that you are rude. You could use the same modal verbs you would use in a formal "face-to-face" situation. Sometimes the words such as "could" or "may" are necessary in order to sound polite. Forget that you are speaking into a phone. You are speaking to a person. Please convey through your voice the friendly smile.

Making Calls

Call People at the Best Times

Normally, we don't make phone calls after 10 P.M. or before 8:00 A.M., unless we have emergencies, or we know that our call is expected. If you have to call the others at improper time, don't forget to apologize for the disturbance first.

In the daytime, you might want to choose the best times for your calls, too, especially when you are seeking a favor or doing business. You know from experience how flat your carefully prepared "casual" talk is when you finally reach someone after having tried several times. Try to figure out when the people you want to call will be available. For example, if you want to call the executives and heads of business firms, the best time to call is after 10 A.M. until lunch time, when their mail has been read and rush dictation is out of the way. For most business executives, afternoons are indefinite. There are visitors, conferences, outside appointments, and trips into the plant. This example is offered only as a guide, for not all executives keep the same hours. Try to find the best times for yourself.

Leaving a Message

If you leave a message for someone to call you back, give not only your name but also your telephone number, unless the person calls you frequently and would surely know it. This will save him or his secretary the trouble of checking the caller's ID, whereas it will take you only a second to give it. If you leave the message on the answering machine, be sure to state your name and number slowly and clearly at the start of the message. Otherwise, you will run the risk of being cut off by the machine when you are still rambling on.

In giving a number to someone who is taking your message, the number should be spoken in groups of two, three or four digits at a time, with a slight pause between. For example, "89456723" could be read as "eight nine, four five, six seven, two three." "0"could be read as "zero" or "oh." "2246555" could be read as "double two four,six triple five." When you have given a number to the message carrier and he repeats it to check up, let him know that he heard it right by saying, "Yes, please," or "That's right." If he gets it wrong, say, "No, it's..." and repeat the number more slowly.

Sometimes when the person calls you back, you might be absent at the time the call comes. When you call again, say, "I'm sorry I wasn't here when you called back."

Wrong Number

It's ordinary to dial a wrong number. If the voice of the person who answers is unfamiliar to you, ask politely, "Is this Mr. Chen speaking?" or " Is this 89456723?" Then you will be quickly told whether you have the correct number. It's impolite to ask, "Who is this?" or "What number is this, anyway?" Most of the time, the person answering would like to have his own privacy. He might counter by asking whom you want or who you are, back and forth in the same useless strain.

If you do get the wrong number, apologize sincerely, "I'm sorry. I have dialed the wrong number," then hang up quietly. Don't end the conversation without saying anything, or keep asking the other side of the line, "How could it be? I'm sure I dialed right." Don't forget the person has already been disturbed by your call and he has no responsibility to listen to your complaint.

Answering Calls

Promptness in Answering

You will be showing great consideration by answering your telephone promptly. It will not only save the time of the caller, but also avoid disturbing the others around you by the phone ring. The work you are doing won't be done well while the phone rings. So why not drop it and answer the phone quickly?

Greeting Warmly

It is mentioned at the beginning of this chapter that a voice with a rising inflection will sound pleasant and inviting. You could start with "Good Morning. Harvey Chen's office," or, "Good afternoon. This is Brook Institute." The greeting is "Good Morning" until 12 A.M.; "Good afternoon" until 6 P.M.; "Good Evening," after that, in businesses that remain open later. Simply "Hello" as an answer generally makes the caller wonder, "Is this the Such-and-Such Company? Have I got the right number?" The useless "hello" habit should be discouraged along with "morning," which sounds as if you are

not fully awake to answer the call. You've surely heard some people say it in a tone of utter weariness, some with a yawn at the end—no way to invite a caller to continue the conversation.

Attentiveness While Answering the Phone

Sometimes you might be up to your ears in your work. No matter how busy you are, try to focus on the call, solve the problem and then proceed with your work. It would be very embarrassing if the caller has stopped talking and you don't have the slightest idea what he has said because you were concentrating on your work. It's also impolite to carry on an aside conversation with someone nearby while the caller is talking. The caller will feel that he's been ignored. Be sure to let him know you're listening. Since you can't show this with a nod, a smile, or other body languages, use verbal responses instead: "Yes, I understand." "Of course," and "I see."

Taking Messages

We often take messages for the others while they are away. The secretary takes messages for the boss every day. Remember to put down the message on a piece of paper. Don't rely on your short-term memory. It's unreliable when you have other work filling your mind. Messages should be written plainly, and they should be explicit. Both the caller's name and phone number are indispensable to the message written down. If the caller doesn't give his name clearly, say to him, "I'm sorry, I didn't get your name, would you spell it for me?" Be alert as he spells it, and then repeat the spelling to check up.

A printed form like this will help you take clear messages for the others. You could make your own forms to meet your needs. The paper could be of a bright color, such as bright orange or bright pink.

TO MR./MS _____

DATE _____ TIME _____

WHEN YOU WERE OUT

MR./MS. _____

FROM _____ PHONE _____

TELEPHONED		PLEASE CALL HIM	
CALLED TO SEE YOU		WILL CALL AGAIN	

MESSAGE _____

_____

_____

MESSAGE RECEIVED BY _____

Don't forget to return the calls promptly when you get the messages. On the other hand, if you've taken messages for someone who is not coming back, you could either show the messages to someone who can call back for him, or call the people back by yourself and explain the situation to him. Don't leave the messages on the desk for days and forget all about it. Twenty-four hours is as long as a call can go unreturned without violating good manners.

If you have a message, but you're really busy that day and could not afford a long conversation, call the person back and arrange another callback time. It will be convenient for both of you.

Screening Calls

Sometimes you would be too busy to answer every call, or you just don't want to be disturbed by strangers or by some particular people. Under this circumstance, you could screen calls by yourself or by the secretary. Identifying the caller's ID on the phone's display is one way to screen calls. But most of the time, phones have to be picked up before the callers are identified. Don't ask the caller "Who is calling?", then tell him "Mr. Chen is not at the office." The caller would be provoked because he knows he's been screened. Technically, as the secretary, you could answer the phone by saying "This is Mr. Chen's Office. Can I help you?" If the answer is, "I'd like to speak to Mr. Chen." You can say, further, "Mr. Chen has asked me to take all his calls first. I'll be very glad to give him any message when I see him later." After getting the caller's identification, if you think Mr. Chen might want to talk with the caller, you could give the message to him and he could call back in a few minutes.

Being Interrupted on the Phone

If You Are Disconnected

There could be many reasons for the disconnection of the calls. It's courteous for you to call the person right back if you are the caller. If the other person put in the call, he should call you. If he does not call you again in two minutes, then you can call him.

If Other People Interrupt Your Call

Your call could be easily interrupted by the other people. For example, you might suddenly be summoned to the boss' office. You could tell the person you are busy now and arrange the time for another call. If your call is interrupted by a colleague or a friend who comes to your office, you could stop the conversation on the phone at an appropriate moment and say, "Will you excuse me for a minute? There's someone on the door." Then quickly make clear to yourself why the other person is in the office. You could tell the visitor that you'll see him later and continue the call with "Sorry to keep you waiting."

If the Phone Interrupts Your Talk

If the phone rings and interrupts your talk with someone, don't pick up the phone while you're still having the original conversation. The caller might overhear the last words of your talking. He would get the feeling that you're very busy and that his call won't get your full attention.

In a Private Office

If you're in someone's private office and your conversation is interrupted by the phone call he receives, should you remain or leave? It depends. If he says to the person on the line, "May I call you back?", you could remain seated. It's obvious he thinks the conversation with you is more important. If he does not, you should start to rise from your chair and ask, "Shall I step out?" He'll probably say, "Oh, no, stay right there. I'll only be a minute." Then you could stay. If he says, "If you don't mind, thank you." Step out of the office and wait. It won't take long. The man you are visiting will come out and invite you again by saying, "Thank you for waiting. I'm sorry we were interrupted."

A Second Call Is Coming

Being interrupted by a second call is common when we are talking on the phone. If you haven't finished the conversation, but you'd like to take the second call, apologize to the first caller and say you'll return immediately. Put him on hold and quickly explain to the other caller that you have to call back. Don't start a conversation with the other caller. Your responsibility is to the first caller, who should never be left on hold for more than thirty seconds. If the incoming call is extremely urgent or from overseas, explain to your first caller why you must hang up and set the time you'll call back.

Closing a Call

If you want to end a call, don't feel uneasy about it. Leaving matters hanging will only waste your time. You could naturally close your call with a conclusive statement: "Ok, I think we all agree this work could be completed ahead of schedule. Shall we talk again, maybe tomorrow?" or "I've had a clue of this project. I'll call you back when I need the details." After that, you could end the conversation with "It's really nice talking to you. Good-bye! " or "Have a nice day."

Who Hangs up First?

It is considered courteous to let the person who is called hang up first or a lady hang up first when she has been talking with a gentleman. If the talk is between you and a customer, let the customer hang up first. But this courtesy is not imposed. If the two people have finished talking and have said good-bye, they are not usually sticklers about this fine point. What is more important is to put the phone down gently. It's discourteous to slam a receiver and deafen the other.

Handling Complaints

If your job is after-sale customer service, or if you have a friend who often calls you and complains about his work, you have to learn how to deal with the complaints on the phone.

Listen Patiently and Don't Interrupt

People call you because they have to find someone to talk with. If you stop them, you might irritate or frustrate them. By letting a person finish his story to his fullest satisfaction, you'll find it easy to calm him down, even though you might provide no actual help at all.

Be Sympathetic

By saying "I'm very sorry. I'll see what I can do for you." or "Cheer up. You've got my support" to the caller, you'll make him feel that his call has been given full attention.

Finding Suitable Places for Phones

In the Street

While making the phone calls, you'd better create a good spot to hold the phone conversation. If you are in a busy street, it is wise to get away from that setting to avoid yelling at the phone. Just remember: It's you, not your phone mate, who is contending with traffic noise. Go into a private area where there are no distractions. If you have to make the phone calls in the street, try to stay away from the cars and the rushing pedestrians. You won't pay enough attention to your safety while being distracted by the phone call.

In Other Public Places

It's also considered improper to make phone calls in some other public places, such as the restaurants and the theatres. People come to these places to dine and relax themselves. The noise of the phone rings is really annoying. At business and social meals alike, making or receiving a phone call at the table is both inconsiderate and intrusive. Please switch the phone to a silent or a vibrate mode. If you have to take the call, excuse yourself from the table and take it in the restroom, the lobby, or step outside.

In the Car

If you want to use your phone while you are driving, please pull over to the side of the road. It will slow you down, but it might save your life. More and more car accidents are caused by the use of phone while driving. Carrying on a phone conversation diverts the driver's attention from the road, and driving with only one hand heightens the danger even more. The use of a portable speakerphone, a build-in phone or a wireless headset with Bluetooth technology will lessen the risk. But don't take chances. Your phone conversation in the car endangers not only your life, but also the other innocent people's lives.

Exercises

1. How would you handle a call for someone else when he does not wish to answer the telephone until he knows who is calling?

2. If you are talking with someone in person and your telephone rings, what courtesy do you show toward the person with you?

3. If someone else answers the telephone and it develops that the call is for you, what should you do if you have to leave a visitor to answer it?

4. If the phone rings while you're driving, how would you answer it?

5. Do you know how to fill in the message form?

Suppose you are Mr. Jackson's colleague. At two o'clock, while Mr. Jackson is out, you receive a call from Ms. Buffet, who is the shop assistant at ABC Bookstore. She wants to inform Mr. Jackson that the book he ordered is now available and he could pick it up anytime in this week. The store's phone number is 89456723. Please write a message for Mr. Jackson.

TO MR./MS _____

DATE _____ TIME _____

WHEN YOU WERE OUT

MR./MS. _____

FROM _____ PHONE _____

TELEPHONED		PLEASE CALL HIM	
CALLED TO SEE YOU		WILL CALL AGAIN	

MESSAGE _____

_____

_____

MESSAGE RECEIVED BY _____

Chapter IX

Correspondence Etiquette

In a narrow sense, business writing refers to the writing that carries business intention only. This kind of writing includes contracts, agreements, letters of intention, commercial notes, telegrams and telecommunication, etc. In a broader sense, business writing may cover any writing that bears both commercial and social function, including business letters. In terms of the etiquette in business writing, this book focuses on business letters, namely etiquette of business correspondence.

Section One   Basic Structure of Business Letters

I. TYPES OF BUSINESS LETTERS

The major types of business letters that we may encounter are (Letters of) Application for a Position and Resume; Letters of Invitation; Letters of Complaints, of Thanks, and of Apologies; Obituary Notice and Letters of Condolence.

1. Letters of Application for a Position and Resume

LETTERS OF APPLICATION FOR A POSITION

A letter of application usually includes the writer's work and education experience, skills, publications, etc. The application is trying to leave a good impression so as to get an interview opportunity.

Sample

July 25, 2004

Foreign Affairs Office
Hefei Union College
Hefei, Anhui Province
P. R. of China

To Whom It May Concern:

I am a graduate student at the Graduate School of Hawaii University concentrating my studies on the People's Republic of China. Upon graduation, I would like to come to your country as an English instructor or tutor.

I have been studying the Chinese language and culture for the past ten months and will continue to study until I graduate in August of 2005. I would then like to continue my studies in China as an English instructor. In addition to my extensive educational background, I have computer and basketball coaching experience which may also be of benefit to you.

Enclosed is a resume highlighting my educational background.

I look forward to your reply. Please feel free to respond in Chinese characters.

Sincerely yours,

John W. White
The Graduate School
Hawaii University
P. O. Box 553
Hawaii

RESUME

Structure of a Resume

Typically a resume consists of

- personal information
- job objective
- qualifications
- work experience
- education
- technical qualifications/ special skills/ key skills
- publications and patents
- social activity
- honors & awards
- references
- conclusion/ summary/ personal statement

Types of Resumes

There are two types of resumes: the chronological resume and the functional resume.

Chronological Resume

Actually this should be called the reverse resume for it lists the jobs you've had going backward in time, from the current one to your first.

Functional Resume

A functional resume describes your skills, abilities and accomplishments as they relate to the job you seek.

Styles of Resumes

A resume can be created in either literal style or form style.

Literal Style

Literal style is a style used in most cases.

Form Style

This style is for the resume that contains less content.

Samples of Resumes

Sample Chronological Resume

MICHAEL COLLINS

4620 Carroll Street
Laramie, WY 82002
(307)555-1212

OBJECTIVE

Join a leading company in the HVAC industry in a key sales-management position, with responsibility for sales and service administration in both domestic and international markets.

SUMMARY

Over 8 years of customer service and inside sales experience in the HVAC industry, with emphasis on hydronic systems and mechanical components. Advance training in the application of chillers, boilers, pumps, and related equipment.

EXPERIENCE

2003—present Manager of Customer Service, Cool Breeze, Inc., Laramie, WY

Key responsibilities include processing of all orders, dealing with representatives on technical issues, coordinating deliveries with production, and reviewing all purchase orders and other legal documents. Initiated regular weekly meetings with purchasing and production departments to

---

reduce lead time on orders. Recognized as employee of year 2004.

1999—2002 Manager of Warranty, Cool Breeze, Inc.

Reviewed all incoming claims under the standard warranty policy. Approved payments or arranged for appropriate action. Reported to senior management on a weekly basis a summary of all claims and reported any critical areas of concern or developing trends to the Engineering and Corporate Safety Coordinator. Reduced the cost of warranty claims by 35% compared to budget for 3 years running.

KEY SKILLS

Experienced in telephone sales

Good working knowledge of order entry

Proficient in use of Internet and Excel, Word, and PowerPoint

EDUCATION

Bachelor of Business Administration , University of Wyoming (1999)

Associate Degree in HVAC systems design and operations, Holbein Institute (1996)

Certificate in advanced air-conditioning repair, Vo-Tech of Laramie (1993)

Summer intern, Hot Stuff Pump Company (1994). Worked with Chief Engineer on the development of a new heat exchange. Prepared drawings using AutoCAD 13. Earned 60% of funds needed for college expenses.

Using the chronological resume style, this manager in the heating, ventilation, and air conditioning (HVAC) business is looking for a higher position in another company. Because he is experienced, he focuses his resume on his work and then lists his educational background at the end. His track record shows him to be a self-reliant person who continues to advance.

Sample Functional Resume

THERSA MONTALVO

211 Elmmond Drive

Houston, tx 77110

(713) 555-1212

OBJECTIVE

Entry level position in accounting, where exceptional math skills, mastery of applicable software, attention to detail, a willingness to work hard, and a positive attitude are required.

EDUCATION

Currently enrolled in night classes at University of Houston, working toward degree in accounting that will enable me to reach my goal of becoming a CPA.

Graduated in 2002 from Hillsboro Junior College, in top 15 percent of class.

EXPERIENCE

2003 to present Assistant Bookkeeper, Moonbeam Computers, Katy, TX
- Created linked spreadsheets to track travel and entertainment using Excel
- Maintained an Access database to record additions to fixed assets
- Downloaded mainframe queries to Excel for account analysis
- Designed an information systems improvement that made cost reports available 20 percent sooner

SUMMARY

Creative problem solver who works well with people. Fluent in Spanish. In junior college, awarded Moore Math Medal two years in a row.

Using the functional resume style, this aspiring accountant shows she's serious by including her eventual goal in her resume—to become a CPA. Because her experience is thin, she first details her education, then specifies her duties in bulleted entries, with the last showing her as the kind of person who does more than is required. The inclusion of her math award backs up her claim to superior math skills.

Principles of Resume

Resume is a critical means in job seeking, and also the first checkpoint to get the employment opportunity. To lessen the chance of your resume being directed toward the wastebasket or deleted with a click of the mouse, be mindful of these basics:

• Be brief and easy to read

A "quick take" shows consideration of the reader's time, a fundamental of business etiquette.

• Be to-the-point and attractive

Illustrate your skills and abilities by relating and outstanding your specific accomplishments instead of merely listing the jobs you held.

• Be error-free

Words are the basic building blocks of writing, and grammar is the blueprint. Your audience may form a certain opinion of you by your blueprint. Furthermore, being

error-free shows respect to the reader, which can be also viewed as etiquette in correspondence.

• Tell the truth

Make certain your resume and cover letter are completely accurate and a true reflection of your experiences. This is a cardinal rule for the job applicant: Don't even think of lying or exaggerating anything in a resume or cover letter. Assume that the truth will come out and have severe, even lifelong, consequences.

Letters of Invitation

The language style of an invitation should be brief and sincere. The main contents may include the reason of invitation, time and place of the activity.

Sample

---

19 October, 1994

Chen Huaming
Institute of Mathematics
Anhui Normal University
Wuhu 241000 China

Dear Professor Chen:

I am pleased to learn that you have the opportunity to spend one year away from your institution to pursue research in atmospheric sciences, and that you would like to spend that year working in my research group at the University of Toronto, I am sure this will be beneficial for both of us. I am therefore happy to invite you to be a Visiting Professor in our department, for one year, beginning any time in the period 1 September 1995—31 December 1995. I understand that the Chinese government will cover the costs of your living expenses while in Toronto. I am happy to provide office space, access to computer facilities, and minor research costs (e.g. photocopying, mail). If any joint work arose then I would also cover publication costs and travel to conferences to present the work (this would be discussed on a case basis).

I look forward to working with you.

Yours faithfully,

Lynn MacDowell
Associate Professor of Physics

---

3. Letters of Complaints, of Thanks and of Apologies

LETTERS OF COMPLAINTS

A letter of complaints should offer clear information about the cause, the date of the affair, the inconveniences or damages caused by that, and it should also propose the remedy for that.

Sample

Dear Sirs,

Your goods for 200 sets of machines arrived yesterday. We found with surprise that the quantity was wrong, short for 7 sets.

This is the first time in all our transactions that you make such mistake. We hope you can do your best to remedy it. We ask you to ship the seven sets on receipt of this letter.

Yours faithfully,

(Signature)

LETTERS OF THANKS

Timing is absolutely important in expressing thanks. In addition, a thank-you letter should be a letter of sincerity and proper diction.

Sample 1

September 1, 1994

Dear Professor _____

Many many thanks for your kind hospitality and the honor you showed me during our delegation's recent visit to your university. It was so nice of you to introduce me so many famous professors and celebrated scholars at your university. We had a safe and sound trip home. Now we have resumed our work.

I hope you will put a short visit to our university and give some lectures on Modern Western Economics this fall.

Please let me know if you want me to do something in China. I look forward to seeing you soon.

With best wishes.

Sincerely yours,

—————————

Direcotr, Foreign Affair Office
Hefei Polytechnical University

Sample 2

May 26, 1994

Dear Professor Smith:

Thank you very much for the great favor you did for me, and the kind interest you took in me.　I am glad to tell you that by your persuasive recommendation I have obtained the position I applied here in the Microsoft Company.　I shall exert my best efforts in performing any duties. I will try to be worthy of your kindness and assistance.

My best regards.

Respectfully yours,
(Signature)

LETTERS OF APOLOGIES

An apology should be made on time.　An honest attitude and a humble style are needed for a letter of apology.

Sample 1

April 14, 2004

Dear Sir:

I am terribly sorry that I wasn't able to come to the class this morning owing to a severe attack of illness. I enclose a certificate from the doctor who is attending me, and he fears it will be several days before I can attend classes.

I hope that my enforced absence will not bother you.

Respectfully yours,

(Signature)

Sample 2

February 22

Dear Henry:

It was not until I got the office this morning that I realized this was Tuesday and I had missed our lunch date Monday. The peaked hat you will see me wearing next time we meet will have "Dunce" written across the band.

I honestly don't know how it happened, since I had been looking forward to seeing you all week. Can you make it for lunch next Monday at the same place? I'll be there at one o'clock unless I hear from you.

Yours ever,
Peter

4. Obituary Notice and Letters of Condolence
OBITUARY NOTICE

What should be declared clearly by an obituary notice includes the dead person's name, identification, position, title, work experience, and the cause, date and place of the death. Honest, sincere and serious language style should be adopted.

Sample 1

Obituary

_____ , vice president of the _____ University, died of lung cancer at 11:30 on June 6, 2007 in No. 1 Hospital at the age of 74 after failing to respond to meticulous medical treatment.

_____ , dedicated all his life to the construction and development of the school. We are deeply grieved over his death.

It is decided that last respects will be paid to his remains at a mourning ceremony on June 11, 2007. Those who want to present wreaths and elegiac couplets come to the Office of Trade Union.

The Funeral Committee for
the Late _____
June 8, 2007

Sample 2

Obituary

Mr and Mrs Relex Water

exceedingly regret to announce

the accidental death of their daughter

Susan Water

on the 24th of August, 1991

while skiing in Sand Mountain

The funeral service will be held

at 4:00 p. m. , Friday, 28th of August, 1991

at Ladbroke Church

LETTERS OF CONDOLENCE

Remember a letter of condolence is not a reminder of the death fact to the family of the dead.

Sample

July 24

Dear Barbara:

We just heard you had lost your mother this morning. John and I know the suddenness of it must have been a dreadful shock. And we just can't tell you how sorry we are.

As all friends of hers know, she was really a great woman. We shall always remember her kindness and goodness. I wish there were something I can do to soften your grief.

Affectionately,

Jean

II. PARTS OF A BUSINESS LETTER

Whichever type of business letter you are going to write, you must organize it into some similar parts. Generally speaking, parts of a business letter can be divided into the main parts and the special parts. The former are the regular parts that every letter has, including the heading (the letterhead / the return address / the sender's address), the dateline, the inside address, the salutation, the body, the closing and the signature; while the latter refer to the parts that can be omitted by business letters, but sometimes these optional parts are necessary or wanted by the writer, including special mailing notations, on-arrival notations, the reference line/notations, the attention line, the subject line, the company signature, the title or section name, the identification line, the enclosure, copies to (cc/carbon copy) and postscript.

The following sample letter is to help you visualize each specific part of a business letter.

Sample Letter   **Part**

◆ KOBE STEEL, LTD.

5-5 Takatsukadai 1-chome, Nishi-ku   1
Kobe, Hyogo 651-2271 JAPAN

November 10, 1999   2

CERTIFIED MAIL   3

CONFIDENTIAL   **4**

Ref: MHI/KSL 10/90   5

Soren Construction Co.   6
4335 Broadway
Indianapolis, IN 46305
USA

Attention: Mr Charles Graham   7
or
ATTENTION: MR CHARLES GRAHAM

Dear Sir,   8

Subject: Rough Terrain Crane RK 250-II   9
Or
SUBJECT: ROUGH TERRAIN CRANE RK 250-II

We have received your inquiry of October 12 concerning our Rough Terrain   10
Crane for your construction project in Chicago, Illinois.
Enclosed please find our brochures explaining the various features of this versatile machine. For an operation the size of yours, I would highly recommend

this model.

If you have any questions that are not covered in the brochures, please do not hesitate to write again, or get in touch with our local representative, Mr. Kevin Walker.

Thank you again for your interest in our products. We look forward to serving you in the future.

Sincerely yours,   11

KOBE STEEL, LTD.   12

Peter Monet

Peter Monet   13
Sales Representative   14

PM:dap   15
Enc: Brochures   16
cc: Mr Kevin Walker   17

Postscript/PS: New Brochures are coming soon.   18

1. Main Parts

THE HEADING (see sample letter part 1)

Letters with the the return (or sender's) address are usually sent by individuals; business to business letters are written on letterhead stationery.

If you do **NOT** use letterhead stationery, the heading includes the writer's complete mailing address and the date. E.g.:

Return Address

Fine Foods Ltd.
10 Bridge Street
London
SW10 5TG

Mr. R. Jones
Sales Manager

If you **DO** use letterhead stationery, the address is already printed on the paper, including
   a) Company name*

b) Street address or post office box number

c) City, state, ZIP code

d) Area code and phone number*

e) Cable address or fax*

*Letterhead only (Do not include your name or phone number in the return address)

THE DATELINE (see sample letter part 2)

The dateline consists of the day, month, and year. The month and year should be spelled out in full, and all numbers should be written as numerals (January 1, not Jan. 1, or January 1st; 2005, not '05). Do not use figures as they can be confusing. In the US the date starts with the month and in Europe, with the day. All the rules are impossible to follow, so just try to work out some rules for yourself. But whether you start with the month or not, do not abbreviate it—this rule stands. If you are using a letterhead, type the date of your letter two to six lines below it depending on the length of the letter. If you are an individual using your return address in the business letter, leave just one line between the return address and the date. In British style of letter writing, sometimes the dateline is written on second line below the inside address.

a) October 6, 20xx (not Oct. 6th)

b) 6 October 20xx (Military or European style)

c) Fixed: Type on third line below letterhead at left margin or beginning at center line

d) Floating: Date line position varies with length of letter.

e) Personal business letters with no printed letterhead: type as last line of return address.

THE INSIDE ADDRESS (see sample letter part 6)

The inside address is typed on fifth line below date line or on third line below any notation(s) following date line. It contains **addressee's courtesy title and full name, addressee's business title when required, name of the business,** and **full address.**

Addressee's courtesy title and full name

A phone inquiry to the addressee's firm to confirm his or her gender will save potential embarrassment. When writing to a woman you don't know, you can address her as "Ms." If you cannot discover the gender of the person, you should drop the courtesy title in the address and salutation. It is awkward, but better than risking an unintended insult. If the addressee holds a doctoral degree, you will need to do some research to decide whether he or she uses the courtesy title "Dr." (Some Ph.D. holders revere their hard-earned title, while others dispense with it entirely.)

Addressee's business title

When an individual holds more than one position in a company, your decision to use all titles or just one will depend on the purpose of the letter and the addressee's

preference. Do not substitute a business title for a courtesy title, however: Address your letter to "Mr. Richard Lambert, President, Alpha Company," not "President Richard Lambert."

Name of the business

It is extremely important to write the name of the business exactly. Look for details: Is "Company /Corporation /Incorporated" spelled out or abbreviated? Does the company name include commas, hyphens, periods, or ampersands? Are words running together? Which letters are capitalized? Find out by checking letterhead, corporate publications, the firm's website or the phone book.

Full address

In the address, numbers are generally written in numeral form unless they are part of the name of a building (One Town Plaza). As a rule, street numbers are written in numerals (123 East 17th Street), yet First through Twelfth are often written in full. Add the letters d, st, or th to numbers over 12 that represent street names. Also, spell out any number that may cause confusion. Preferably, spell out street, avenue, building, and directional words such as east and northwest. City names are written in full unless an abbreviation is the accepted spelling (St. Louis). Foreign addresses should conform to the standards in the country of the addressee. The ZIP code is typed on the same line as city and state, with two spaces between state and ZIP left.

Other General Tips on the Inside Address

- Write the name exactly as the person or business does in her/his/its correspondence to you. For example:
- Include addressee's job title and department if known.
- Avoid double titles.
- Break a long company name into two lines for balance.
- Preferably, inside and outside addresses are the same and include addressee's name and job title, name of organization, street address or post office box number, city, state, and ZIP.

and

- For a letter to a business, the address line includes the following:
    - ☐ Full name of the business
    - ☐ Department name, if necessary

    and

    - ☐ Full address

THE SALUTATION (see sample letter part 8)

All letters begin with a salutation or greeting. The salutation is typed on second line below inside address (or attention line if used). In most cases it is a simple "Dear Mr. /Dr. ____," followed by a colon/or a comma. A first name is used only when you know the addressee well or you and the addressee have agreed to correspond on a first-name basis.

What to write when you are addressing a company rather than an identifiable person? "Sir or Madam" and "Ladies and Gentlemen" sound stilted; "To whom it may concern" is acceptable but rather formal and clichéd. The best solution is probably to address the company ("Dear Blue Sky Investments") or department ("Dear Investor Relations") or to direct your salutation to a specific position ("Dear Human Resources Director").

Other General Tips on Salutation

- Salutation must agree in number with the first line of the inside address.
- When you've used an attention line, the letter is considered addressed to the whole organization rather than to the person named on the attention line. Hence, the correct salutation is "Ladies and Gentlemen", not "Dear Mr. Name-In-Attention-Line."
- When you are addressing a firm or a group of men you can use "Gentlemen".
- Use of the correct title is important. Look at the chart below:

ADDRESSEE	AMERICAN STYLE	BRITISH STYLE
Tom Smith	Dear Mr. Smith:	Dear Mr Smith,
Susan Fox. PhD	Dear Dr. Fox:	Dear Dr Fox,
Mary Lane	Dear Ms. Lane:	Dear Ms Lane,

Note that the American style has a period after the title (Mr. Dr. Ms.). It also uses a colon (:). The British style does not have a period after the title and uses a comma (,). Ms. or Ms (pronounced Miz) is now in common use as a female equivalent to Mr. However, if possible, it is best to find out which title the woman herself prefers (Ms. or Mrs. or Miss). All of the examples above are in formal style which should be used for all business letters. Use of the first name (Dear Tom, Dear Sue, etc) is only for informal, personal letters.

THE BODY (see sample letter part 10)

The top priority for a business letter is brevity. It should not go beyond one page unless absolutely necessary. Therefore, be sure to be concise and to the point but never discourteous.

At the beginning you usually need to mention the letter from the other party in a brief way so as to make the recipient know to which letter your letter respond. If it is the first-time correspondence you can make a brief introduction of yourself and your purpose.

A complete sentence as the close is needed for a formal letter while an incomplete sentence is allowed in an informal letter.

Hints on structure

<u>Expressing thanks for a favor done</u>

to someone who invited you somewhere...	Thank you for inviting me to...
to someone who called you...	Thank you for calling me...
to someone who took you to dinner...	Thank you for taking me to dinner...
to someone who helped you...	Thank you for helping me with...

Writing about future events

you plan to meet someone	I look forward to meeting you...
you want to receive a reply	I look forward to your reply...
you plan to visit someone	I look forward to my visit...
someone plans to visit you	I look forward to your visit...
you plan to attend a conference	I look forward to the conference..

When writing to someone you have not met, let the person know why you are familiar with him or her.

you saw someone's presentation	I had the pleasure of attending your presentation at...
you read someone's article	I read your article in the .... with interest...
you saw someone's poster session	I had the opportunity to see your poster session at ...
you participated in someone's workshop	I had the pleasure of participating in your workshop at ...

When asking for a favour, leave the person as much time as possible. Nevertheless, if you expect to have a reply within a certain time, make that request specific.

Please let us know as soon as possible.
Please call by the end of July
Please visit us at your earliest convenience.
Please reply by fax before September 10.

Referral Statements

telephone	Please do not hesitate to telephone us...
get in touch	Please get in touch with our representative in...
send further enquiries	Please send further enquiries to... at the following address...
contact	Please contact... at the following address...

Tone

A business relationship can often become fairly informal. If you find yourself in this situation, you can alter the tone of your business correspondence from **impersonal to personal**.

Impersonal	Personal
Thank you very much (for your help) ...	Thanks a lot (for your help) ...

I appreciated (your recommendations) ...	Thanks for (your recommendations) ....
Please give my regards to (your secretary) ...	Tell (your secretary) I said 'Hello' ...
I look forward to (seeing you next month) ...	It'll be good to (see you next month) ...

Margin Guide

Letter Length	Width of Margins (cm)	Line Length (cm)
Long	2.5	16.25
Medium	3.75	13.75
Short	5	11.25

Other General Tips on the Body Part

- Leave single space within but double space between paragraphs.
- Place on page based on letter length, visualizing "frame" of white space around letter. Bottom margin should be at least six lines deep.

THE CLOSING/THE COMPLEMENTARY CLOSE (see sample letter part 11)

A complimentary close is typed on second line below last line of the main body of your letter, followed by a comma. It is a conventional expression, indicating the formal close of the letter. The first word is capitalized. For a formal close, you may use one of the variations of "Truly" ("Yours truly": BrE; "Truly yours": AmE). If you and your addressee are on a first-name basis, closings such as "As ever," "Best wishes," "Regards," "Kindest regards" will be quite acceptable. Closings such as "Respectfully" and "Respectfully yours" which are often seen in diplomatic and ecclesiastical writing, are too obsequious for most business letters.

	American Style	British Style
Very Formal	Respectfully, Respectfully yours,	Yours respectfully,
Formal	Sincerely, Sincerely yours,	Sincerely, Sincerely yours,
Informal	All the best, Regards,	Best wishes, All the best,

THE SIGNATURE (see sample letter part 13)

Ordinarily, the typed name is on fourth line below the company signature (if used) or the complimentary closing (if letter is short, leave up to six lines blank for signature; if long, reduce to two blank lines), beginning at the same point as complimentary closing or company signature. Every letter should have a handwritten signature before the typed one.

Signature should be in the form by which the writer wishes to be addressed. Your signature may show your preference in courtesy title. A woman may include "Miss",

"Mrs." or "Ms." to the right of the typewritten signature. A man, however, should not include "Mr." in his signature unless he uses only initials or has a name that could also be a woman's:

e.g. Mr. J.G. Eberle or Mr. Lynn Treadway

A secretary who signs a letter at the boss's request customarily signs the boss's name, followed by his / her own initials.

If the writers of a letter are more than one, the signatures can be blocked together either vertically or side by side.

Be sure that not only the complimentary close and the signature should be seen on the same page, but also should not be the only content on this page, otherwise the writer is considered discourteous.

2. Special Parts

THE SPECIAL MAILING NOTATIONS (see sample letter part 3)

The manuals on business correspondence recommend to type special mailing notations in all uppercase characters before the inside address.

THE ON-ARRIVAL NOTATIONS(see sample letter part 4)

You might want to include a special notation on private correspondence. This is also typed in all uppercase characters or you could prefer to bold them before the inside address (after the special mailing notation if you have included it too). Others prefer to put it between the inside address and the salutation. Remember to put it on the envelope as well, which is probably even more important.

THE REFERENCE LINE/NOTATIONS(see sample letter part 5)

This consists of the word Ref (short for Reference) followed by a colon (:) and specific information, often a serial or reference number. It is usually placed between the date and the inside address.

When the guide words "When replying, refer to" are not printed on the letterhead but are desired, type on the second line below the date line or below any notations that follow it, and type your appropriate reference number or filing code two spaces after the colon:

When replying, refer to: CD-1703

When replying to a letter that contains a reference number, type a reference notation on the second line below the date line or below any notation after it:

In reply to: G2467 Or Refer to: G 2467

When you must give both your and the addressee's reference, type yours first (as in above), skip a line, and type his or hers. For example:

When replying, refer to: CD 1703

Or

Your reference: G 2467

Some writers prefer to give addressee's reference notation as a subject line (see subject line).

THE ATTENTION LINE (see sample letter part 7)

When a letter is addressed to a company or organization rather than an individual, an attention line may be given to help in mail delivery. The attention line contains the word Attention (or Attn) followed by a colon (:) and the name of the office, department or individual. It is placed between the inside address and the salutation, on second line below inside address. The word attention is typed in all capitals or in capital and small letters, number abbreviated, not underlined, and followed by a colon. Attention lines are typically directed to: Sales Division, Personnel Manager, etc. or it may contain the individual's name.

An attention line is never given when the inside address contains a person's name. Many companies now omit the attention line and type the name of the person or department above the company name in the inside address. Whenever possible, omit the attention line. Address the letter directly to an individual in the organization, by name and title.

THE SUBJECT LINE (see sample letter part 9)

The subject line is used to immediately draw the reader's attention to the subject of the letter. It consists of the word Subject followed by a colon (:) and a word or words of specific information. The position of the subject line is not standardized. It may appear to the right of the inside address, or centered on the page below the inside address or below the salutation. It is commonly placed between salutation and body, with one blank line above and below, either typed in capital and small or in all-capital letters, not underlined.

THE COMPANY SIGNATURE (see sample letter part 12)

The company signature is used to emphasize that a letter represents the views of the company as a whole, not just the company employee who wrote it. It is typed in all capitals on second line below complimentary closing, beginning at same point as complimentary closing.

THE TITLE OR SECTION NAME (see sample letter part 14)

This is placed one space below the typewritten signature to identify the writer's position and / or the section he / she works in and it also helps to achieve a good visual balance.

THE IDENTIFICATION LINE/REFERENCE INITIALS (see sample letter part 15)

When the person whose signature appears on the letter is not the person who typed the letter, there is an identification line. It consists of two sets of initials separated by a colon. Usually, the sender's initials are capitalized and the typist's are in lower case. The identification line is two spaces below the signature and even with the left margin. If the writer's name is typed in the signature block, type the typist's initials alone on the second line below the writer's name and title. If the writer wants his / her

initials included, they precede the typist's.

When someone other than the person who signs it writes the letter, the writer's and the typist's (not the signer's and the typist's) initials are written.

THE ENCLOSURE (see sample letter part 16)

When something is enclosed with the letter, an enclosure line is usually below the identification line. If there is no identification line, the enclosure line is on second line below the signature. It is usually written Enclosure or Enc followed by a colon (:) and information. The enclosures should always be referred to in the body of the letter. It is wise to include the number of enclosures and (when necessary for legal purposes) to identify each by name.

COPIES TO (CC/CARBON COPY) (see sample letter part 17)

When a copy of a letter is sent to another person, the letters cc followed by a colon (:) and the name of the person to whom the copy is being sent is typed below the enclosure line (or the identification line if there are no enclosures). If there is no identification line, it appears on second line below the signature. The letters "cc" traditionally stand for "carbon copy". If several people are to receive copies, type their names below the first name, arranged by rank or alphabetically. Don't repeat cc or c. When using both first names and/or initials with last names, omit personal titles except in formal letters and/or if using nicknames with last names.

Note this distinction:

cc: Mr. R.R. Parent (received only copy of letter)

Cc/enc: Mr. T.W. Baldwin (received copies of letter and enclosure)

Postscript

Use a postscript for emphasis to express effectively an idea that you have deliberately withheld from the body of the letter. Type flush left or indented (according to body paragraph format) on second line below what was typed last, beginning with no abbreviation at all or one of these: PS: or PS.

3. Second Page

The second page of a business letter is typed with plain paper (never a letterhead), using same margins as on first page. The second page heading is typed on the seventh line down from top of page, giving addressee's name, page number, and date. On the third line below last line of heading, resume letter. There are at least two lines of a paragraph at the bottom—and at the top—of the next page. It is not advisable to have just the complimentary closing on the last page or divide the last word on a page.

4. A Few Additional Points

PUNCTUATION OF ADDRESSES

It has become common to use open punctuation, especially in a full block business letter. It means no punctuation at all at the end of the address lines. If you prefer to use punctuation, follow by a comma each line of the address except the last one.

ABOUT PUNCTUATION

According to the US rules for business letters, you are supposed to use colon (:) after salutation and comma after complimentary close; it is called mixed punctuation. In Europe commas are used in both cases. Open punctuation (i.e. no punctuation) after salutation and complimentary close is becoming common, especially in the US.

ABOUT LINE BREAKS

There used to be strict rules about line breaks between different parts of the letter. For instance, you were supposed to leave two breaks after salutation and two breaks between the body of the letter and the complimentary close. Now these rules are becoming less strict. You can use your own judgment in choosing which rules to follow and to what extent.

III. LAYOUT OF BUSINESS WRITING

1. Types of Layouts

BLOCK STYLE

This style requires each line flush to the left, so the whole eventually flushes to the left as a block.

MODIFIED BLOCK STYLE

Modified block is a traditional and popular format for business letters. The format is appropriate for both paper and electronic correspondence. It places the return address, including the author's name, at the top just right of center, with the date and any referenced subject underneath. The complimentary closing and signature block are at the bottom, again, just right of center. All other parts of the letter are typed flush left, with the right margin not justified. This includes the name and address of the person the letter is being sent to (inside address), the salutation, the correspondence paragraphs (body), and any enclosure notes and courtesy copy notifications. The return address is not included if the letter is printed on letterhead.

MODIFIED SEMI-BLOCK STYLE OR INDENTED STYLE

The indented or modified semi-block style of business letters is very similar to the modified block letters. The only difference between the two is that the indented letters' paragraphs are indented one tab stop.

SEMI-BLOCK STYLE

Some people believe that semi-block style just refers to indented style. According to Wikipedia, however, in a semi-block letter, all text is aligned to the left margin, and paragraphs are indented.

For visualization of these formats, please see the samples in "2."

2. Samples of Different Layouts
BLOCK STYLE

Peter Monet

******* Laboratory

Technical Development Group

Kobe Steel Ltd

5-5 Takatsukadai 1-chome

Nishi-ku

Kobe

Hyogo

Japan 651-2271

November 10, 1999

CERTIFIED MAIL

CONFIDENTIAL

Ref: MHI/KSL 10/90

Soren Construction Co.

4335 Broadway

Indianapolis, IN 46305

USA

ATTENTION: MR CHARLES GRAHAM

Dear Sir,

Subject: Rough Terrain Crane RK 250-II

We have received your inquiry of October 12 concerning our Rough Terrain Crane for your construction project in Chicago, Illinois.

Enclosed please find our brochures explaining the various features of this versatile machine. For an operation the size of yours, I would highly recommend this model.

If you have any questions that are not covered in the brochures, please do not hesitate to write again, or get in touch with our local representative, Mr. Kevin Walker.

Thank you again for your interest in our products. We look forward to serving you in the future.

Sincerely yours,

KOBE STEEL, LTD.

Peter Monet

Peter Monet
Sales Representative

PM:dap
Enc: Brochures
cc: Mr Kevin Walker

Postscript/PS: New Brochures are coming soon.

MODIFIED BLOCK STYLE

Peter Monet
******* Laboratory
Technical Development Group
Kobe Steel Ltd
5-5 Takatsukadai 1-chome
Nishi-ku
Kobe
Hyogo
Japan 651-2271
November 10, 1999

CERTIFIED MAIL

CONFIDENTIAL

Ref: MHI/KSL 10/90

Soren Construction Co.

4335 Broadway
Indianapolis, IN 46305
USA

ATTENTION: MR CHARLES GRAHAM

Dear Sir,

Subject: Rough Terrain Crane RK 250-II

We have received your inquiry of October 12 concerning our Rough Terrain Crane for your construction project in Chicago, Illinois.

Enclosed please find our brochures explaining the various features of this versatile machine. For an operation the size of yours, I would highly recommend this model.

If you have any questions that are not covered in the brochures,   please do not hesitate to write again, or get in touch with our local representative, Mr. Kevin Walker.

Thank you again for your interest in our products.   We look forward to serving you in the future.

Sincerely yours,

KOBE STEEL, LTD.

Peter Monet

Peter Monet
Sales Representative

PM:dap
Enc: Brochures
cc: Mr Kevin Walker

Postscript/PS: New Brochures are coming soon.

MODIFIED SEMI-BLOCK STYLE OR INDENTED STYLE

****** Laboratory

Peter Monet

****** Laboratory

Technical Development Group

Kobe Steel Ltd

5-5 Takatsukadai 1-chome

Nishi-ku

Kobe

Hyogo

Japan 651-2271

November 10, 1999

CERTIFIED MAIL

CONFIDENTIAL

Ref: MHI/KSL 10/90

Soren Construction Co.

4335 Broadway

Indianapolis, IN 46305

USA

ATTENTION: MR CHARLES GRAHAM

Dear Sir,

Subject: Rough Terrain Crane RK 250-II

We have received your inquiry of October 12 concerning our Rough Terrain Crane for your construction project in Chicago, Illinois.

Enclosed please find our brochures explaining the various features of this versatile machine. For an operation the size of yours, I would highly recommend this model.

If you have any questions that are not covered in the brochures, please do not hesitate to write again, or get in touch with our local representative, Mr. Kevin Walker.

Thank you again for your interest in our products. We look forward to serving you in the future.

Sincerely yours,

KOBE STEEL, LTD.

Peter Monet

Peter Monet
Sales Representative

PM:dap
Enc: Brochures
cc: Mr Kevin Walker

Postscript/PS: New Brochures are coming soon.

SEMI-BLOCK STYLE

Peter Monet
******* Laboratory
Technical Development Group
Kobe Steel Ltd
5-5 Takatsukadai 1-chome
Nishi-ku
Kobe
Hyogo
Japan 651-2271
November 10, 1999

CERTIFIED MAIL

CONFIDENTIAL

Ref: MHI/KSL 10/90

Soren Construction Co.

4335 Broadway
Indianapolis, IN 46305
USA

ATTENTION: MR CHARLES GRAHAM

Dear Sir,

Subject: Rough Terrain Crane RK 250-II

We have received your inquiry of October 12 concerning our Rough Terrain Crane for your construction project in Chicago, Illinois.

Enclosed please find our brochures explaining the various features of this versatile machine. For an operation the size of yours, I would highly recommend this model.

If you have any questions that are not covered in the brochures, please do not hesitate to write again, or get in touch with our local representative, Mr. Kevin Walker.

Thank you again for your interest in our products. We look forward to serving you in the future.

Sincerely yours,

KOBE STEEL, LTD.

Peter Monet

Peter Monet
Sales Representative

PM:dap
Enc: Brochures
cc: Mr Kevin Walker

Postscript/PS: New Brochures are coming soon.

IV. ENVELOPE

1. Format

There is approximately 40mm from the upper line of Address to the upper edge of the envelope.

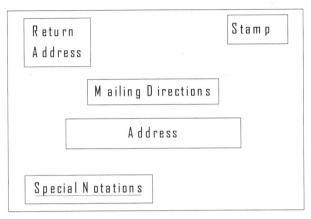

2. Samples

BLOCKED FORM OF ADDRESS

Roman International Inc.
2203 Broadway
New York N.Y. 100101
U.S.A.

         Mr. John Smith
         Astin Asia Ltd.
         30/F Cornwall House
         1000 King's Road
         Hong Kong

CONFIDENTIAL

INDENTED FROM OF ADDRESS

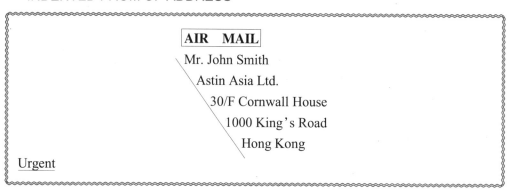

Section Two Principles in and Tips on Composing Business Letters

The myth about business correspondence is that it must be formal, standardized and often terse. The writer seems to transform him / herself from the personal to the institutional. Letters appear to be written from one "institution" to another rather than from person to person. This does nothing more than creating ineffective communication. It is important to develop a good writing style that not only reflects good grammar and sentence structure, but also gives the reader some insight into the personality of the writer. It is just as important, however, to be able to express yourself in clear, concise language so the reader knows exactly why you are writing.

I. PRINCIPLES

Good English letter writing is supposed to cover the following "Five C Principles"

Consideration

Conciseness

Clarity

Courtesy

Correctness

For a business letter, the other "Three C Principles" should be added.

Completeness

Concreteness

Consistency

II. GENERAL TIPS ON BUSINESS CORRESPONDENCE

• Your letter should not be more than one page in length.

• Your letter should be free of spelling and grammatical errors.

- Type all letters on good quality business stationery of A4 size — preferably matching your resume paper
- Use either block style or modified block style.
- Whether write it or type it, use black ink only
- Make the format and layout attractive; center the letter on the page; allow ample margins; make it appealing to look at and inviting to the reader
- Watch your sentence structure; proof read the letter several times to be sure you are saying what you want to say
- Do not send photocopies or generic letters; you can create a model letter which can be used many times with slight revisions
- Do not e-mail or fax any business correspondence (resumes, applications, letters, etc.) unless you are specifically asked to do so. Even then, follow it up with a hard copy in the mail
- Be sure to sign the letter before you mail it
- Buy large envelopes (9x12) instead of matching business envelopes. That way you can mail your resume and cover letter without having to fold or crease them in any way. Be sure to add the extra postage for a large envelope.
- Reply to the letter you have received at your earliest convenience, within a week since the day you received it at the most.

Section Three Etiquette of Informal Business Correspondence

In this section, some general tips on email and fax etiquette are introduced.

I. EMAIL

Email can be an efficient save of time and paper, but because it is so easy and ubiquitous, it is also ripe for abuse. Businesses are being swamped with email to such an extent that productivity is being affected.

A lot can be done to avoid propagating email stress and corporate spam by observing the following points.

- Avoid sending an email unless it is absolutely necessary.
- Avoid sending copies or forwarding emails to persons not directly involved in the subject matter.
- If you must forward an email, delete the parts that are irrelevant to the recipient.
- Think carefully before you decide to click "reply to all."
- Do not request a delivery receipt or that the email has been read unless such information is vital.

- If you reply just to say "thanks" you are contributing to corporate spam. It's courteous, but is it necessary?
- Use the Subject field to concisely and accurately describe the contents.
- Avoid ambiguity to stop a further exchange of emails seeking clarification.
- Keep the contents clear and to the point.
- Does your email really require a reply? If not just end with NRN (no reply necessary).
- Email is not appropriate for formal communications, such as invitations or birth announcements.
- Email is not an excuse for misspellings, grammatical errors, or punctuation mistakes. Your familiarity with such rules should shine through at all times, no matter what medium you use.
- It will be perfectly fine if on-line terms and abbreviations are part of the electronic parlance of the people you do business with; if they aren't, then use of these symbols may mean nothing to the recipient and annoy at the same time.
- When you send group emails, be careful that the program you're using isn't the kind that reveals all of the recipients' email addresses in the address field. Instead, use a program that displays only the address of that specific recipient on each email. Plus, it is dangerous to rely on email for any truly important message because it can easily be duplicated, altered, and forged.
- Make sure email information is included on your resume.
- Follow the same business etiquette in emailing credentials that would be used in mailing a resume.
- Include all closing information on your email message including name, address, telephone, and return email information.
- Reply to the email you have received within 24 hours.

II. FAX

It can be informal at times, but faxing documents is still a business process, so you should always try to follow these business fax etiquette guidelines:

1. Always Use a Cover Page

Even if it's just a handwritten note (although clear, pre-printed material usually works best), include a cover page on each fax. Be sure to clearly note your name and contact number, the number of pages being sent, the name of the intended recipient, and any other pertinent information before transmitting.

FORMAT OF A FAX COVER PAGE

Generally speaking, a FAX Cover Sheet is composed of the heading, the sender's and receiver's contact and the message parts. The heading includes the address, phone and fax number of the sender/the sender's business. The contact includes the respective

names of the sender and the receiver (to & from) and their respective phone numbers and fax numbers. The message part consists of "number of pages", date, subject, comment and message.

	Unitversity Marketing Communication
FAX	1125 Kinnear Road
	Columbus, OH 43212-1153
	Phone (614) 292-4272
	Fax (614) 292-2387

To:	From:
Fax:	Fax:
Phone:	Phone:
No. of pages including this one	Date:
Subj	
Comments:	

Message

2. Follow Up to Confirm

Simply sending a fax doesn't mean that the intended recipient read it, or even received it. Don't assume that unsolicited or unexpected faxes have reached their intended targets. Always follow up to confirm. Make sure your FAX communication is followed by a FAX confirmation of receipt.

3. Practice Discretion

If you're sending confidential or potentially sensitive information, make sure to call ahead and let the recipient know to be ready. Using an online fax service can help avoid security issues, as it lets users send and receive faxes from the privacy of their personal computer screens.

Exercises

1. Write an application letter for a position in a block style. Include at least 10 parts of the components of a business letter. Pay attention to the format of your writing.

2. Create a resume for yourself.

GLOSSARY

adamant	*a.*	坚定不移的,牢不可破的	Chapter 7
adjacent	*a.*	与……毗连的;邻近的	Chapter 7
albeit	*conj.*	尽管,即使	Chapter 7
alter	*v.*	改变	Chapter 9
amiably	*adv.*	和蔼可亲地,亲切地	Chapter 7
ampersand	*n.*	和号,& 的记号名称	Chapter 9
angst	*n.*	焦虑不安,烦恼	Chapter 4
apex	*n.*	顶点;尖端,<喻>顶峰	Chapter 5
appointive	*a.*	由任命而充当的	Chapter 3
aspiring	*a.*	有志气的,有抱负的	Chapter 9
astute	*a.*	机敏的,精明的,狡猾的	Chapter 7
asymmetric	*a.*	不对称的,不匀称的	Chapter 2
attire	*n.*	服装,衣服	Chapter 2
badge	*n.*	徽章,标记,标志,象征	Chapter 5
ballerina	*n.*	芭蕾舞女演员	Chapter 2
bandanas	*n.*	丝制手帕	Chapter 2
barrette	*n.*	(妇女用的)条状发夹	Chapter 2
béchamel	*n.*	贝夏梅尔调味白汁	Chapter 5
Bermuda-length shorts		长度在膝盖以上两三厘米的西裤剪裁型短裤	Chapter 2
bias	*n.*	斜纹;偏见	Chapter 2
bisque	*n.*	(乳脂、番茄等的)浓汤	Chapter 5
blazer	*n.*	宽松运动外衣;夹克	Chapter 2
block style	*n.*	垂直式或齐头式商业文书格式	Chapter 9
boil down to	*v. phr.*	归结为	Chapter 2
Bordeaux	*n.*	波尔多葡萄酒	Chapter 5
bouillon	*n.*	肉汤,牛肉汤	Chapter 5
brash	*a.*	傲慢的,无礼的;轻率的	Chapter 3
brevity	*n.*	短暂,简洁	Chapter 9
brisk	*a.*	轻快的,活泼的;麻利的	Chapter 2
brocade	*n.*	锦缎	Chapter 2
brochure	*n.*	小册子,说明书	Chapter 9
buffer	*n.*	起缓冲作用的人(或物)	Chapter 7
Burgundy	*n.*	勃艮第红葡萄酒;深红色	Chapter 5
Canapés	*n.*	冷盘;小糕点	Chapter 5

carbon copy	n.	复写本,打字副本	Chapter 9
cardiac	a.	心脏(病)的	Chapter 7
cardinal	a.	最重要的,主要的	Chapter 9
cardiopulmonary	a.	<医>心肺的	Chapter 7
caveat	n.	警告,附加说明,告诫	Chapter 2
Chablis	n.	白葡萄酒的一种	Chapter 5
check	n.	方格	Chapter 2
cheongsam	n.	旗袍	Chapter 2
chiffon	n.	雪纺绸	Chapter 2
clam	n.	蚌,蛤	Chapter 5
clamp	n.	夹子	Chapter 2
	v.	夹住,固定	
Claret	n.	波尔多红葡萄酒中的一种	Chapter 5
cliché	n.	老生常谈,陈词滥调	Chapter 9
Cobb salad	n.	考勃沙拉(以人命名)	Chapter 5
Cognac	n.	科涅克白兰地(法)	Chapter 5
complimentary close	n.	信尾问候语	Chapter 9
concoction	n.	调和物	Chapter 5
condiment	n.	调味品,佐料	Chapter 5
condolence	n.	同情;吊唁	Chapter 3
confection	n.	甜食,糕点	Chapter 5
confidential	a.	秘密的,机密的	Chapter 9
configuration	n.	构造,形状;编排,配置,布局	Chapter 7
consommé	n.	清汤	Chapter 5
consummate	v. a.	使结束,使完美;完美的	Chapter 7
cordial	a.	热诚的,热情友好的	Chapter 3
correspondence	n.	信件,函件	Chapter 9
crème brûlée	n.	焦糖奶油	Chapter 5
crudités	n.	蔬菜色拉	Chapter 5
cummerbund	n.	腹带,徽带,装饰带	Chapter 2
cuticles	n.	角质层	Chapter 2
daunting	a.	使人畏缩的	Chapter 5
decree	n. vt.	命令,法令,颁布……为法令	Chapter 1
defibrillator	n.	(电击)除颤器	Chapter 7
demitasse	n.	小型咖啡杯,小杯清咖啡	Chapter 5
denouement	n.	(戏剧、小说等的)结局	Chapter 5
deterrent	n.	阻碍物	Chapter 7
discreet	a.	(言行)谨慎的,慎重的	Chapter 4
dispense	vt.	施与,提供(尤指服务);分配	Chapter 2

ironclad	*a. n.*	<美> 严格的;装甲舰	Chapter 2
itinerary	*n.*	旅程;行程	Chapter 4
khaki slacks	*n.*	卡其裤	Chapter 2
lapel	*n.*	(西服上衣或夹克的)翻领	Chapter 2
lapse	*n.*	失误,过失;小毛病	Chapter 3
layout	*n.*	布局;安排;版面设计	Chapter 9
limburger	*n.*	林堡干酪(比利时产,气味浓烈)	Chapter 7
linguine	*n.*	(意大利)扁面条	Chapter 5
locale	*n.*	(事件发生的)场所或地点	Chapter 2
lucrative	*a.*	获利多的,赚钱的	Chapter 5
Madeira	*n.*	大西洋的群岛名,该地产的白葡萄酒	Chapter 5
magenta	*a.*	紫红色的;洋红色的	Chapter 2
martyr	*n.*	殉道者;乞怜者(向人诉苦以博取同情)	Chapter 7
matte	*a.*	不光滑的	Chapter 2
mock	*a.*	仿制的;模拟的	Chapter 6
monochromatic	*a.*	单色的,单频的	Chapter 2
morale	*n.*	士气;斗志	Chapter 7
Moselle	*n.*	摩泽尔白葡萄酒	Chapter 5
nauseous	*a.*	令人作呕的;讨厌的	Chapter 7
nickelodeon	*n.*	五分钱戏院	Chapter 5
notation	*n.*	记号	Chapter 9
notoriously	*adv.*	恶名昭彰地;众所周知地	Chapter 5
nuance	*n.*	微妙的色彩;细微差别	Chapter 3
obituary	*n.*	讣告,讣闻	Chapter 9
oblong	*n. a.*	长方形;长方形的,椭圆形的	Chapter 2
olfactory	*a.*	嗅觉的	Chapter 7
paranoid	*n. a.*	偏执狂;多疑的	Chapter 7
parlance	*n.*	腔调,说法,用语	Chapter 9
pashmina	*n.*	羊绒围巾	Chapter 2
pastry	*n.*	糕点,油酥糕点	Chapter 5
pertinent	*a.*	有关的;中肯的;恰当的	Chapter 9
pithy	*a.*	简练的,精辟的,简洁扼要的	Chapter 5
platinum	*n.*	铂;白金	Chapter 2
pleated	*a.*	打褶裥的,起褶的	Chapter 2
polyester	*n.*	聚酯纤维,涤纶	Chapter 2
preept	*v.*	优先	Chapter 5
proffer	*vt.*	提供,贡献,提出	Chapter 3
propogate	*v.*	繁殖,传播	Chapter 9
protocol	*n.*	礼仪;外交礼仪	Chapter 1

pumps	*n.*	浅口无带皮鞋	Chapter 2
punctuation	*n.*	标点符号	Chapter 9
purées	*n.*	蔬菜泥;水果泥	Chapter 5
reciprocate	*v.*	报答;酬答	Chapter 4
reek	*n. v.*	恶臭;发出难闻的气味	Chapter 7
resuscitation	*n.*	复活;复苏;恢复	Chapter 7
revere	*vt.*	崇敬,尊崇,敬畏	Chapter 9
Rhone	*n.*	罗纳河;以此地命名的葡萄酒	Chapter 5
risqué	*a.*	有伤风化的	Chapter 7
salutary	*a.*	有益的(尽管往往让人不愉快)	Chapter 3
satin	*n.*	缎,缎子	Chapter 2
sauterne	*n.*	白葡萄酒的一种	Chapter 5
savory	*n. a.*	(烹调用的)香薄荷;好吃的	Chapter 5
scoot	*n. v.*	疾走,迅速跑开	Chapter 6
seam	*n.*	缝,接口	Chapter 2
shawl	*n.*	围巾,披肩	Chapter 2
sheaf	*n.*	捆,束,扎	Chapter 2
solid	*n.*	纯色	Chapter 2
soothe	*vt.*	安慰,抚慰,使舒服,使平静	Chapter 4
sorbet	*n.*	果汁冰糕	Chapter 5
sport	*n.*	(用作友好称呼,尤指男子)老兄,朋友,哥们儿	Chapter 3
spurn	*vt.*	一脚踢开;拒绝接受	Chapter 7
stickler	*n.*	坚持……的人	Chapter 8
stilted	*a.*	(动作或言语)生硬的,不自然的	Chapter 9
stole	*n.*	女用披肩	Chapter 2
stud	*n.*	领扣,按扣	Chapter 2
subliminally	*adv.*	下意识地	Chapter 6
tab	*n.*	拉襻;扣环	Chapter 2
taboo	*n.*	禁忌的事物(或行为);禁忌语	Chapter 1
tails	*n.*	燕尾服,男子晚礼服	Chapter 2
take it out on	*sb. v.*	向某人出气	Chapter 4
taupe	*n. a.*	灰褐色;褐色的	Chapter 2
terse	*a.*	(说话、文笔等)精练的,简洁的	Chapter 9
tousled	*a.*	凌乱的	Chapter 2
trample	*v.*	踩,踏;无视;侵犯	Chapter 1
tunic suit	*n.*	中山装	Chapter 2
tuxedo	*n.*	无尾晚礼服	Chapter 2
ubiquitous	*a.*	普遍存在的;十分普遍的	Chapter 9
unobtrusive	*a.*	不引人注目的,谦虚的;不冒昧的	Chapter 4

unsolicited	*a.*	主动提供的	Chapter 9
velouté	*n.*	(一种用黄油和面粉调成的)鲜肉汁酱	Chapter 5
Versailles	*n.*	凡尔赛宫	Chapter 1
vicious	*a.*	邪恶的,残酷的,危险的	Chapter 5
Windsor knot	*n.*	温莎结	Chapter 2
yarn	*n.*	纱,纱线,纺线	Chapter 2

References

Baugh, L. Sue, Fryar, Maridell & Dave Thomas. 1999. *Here's How: Write First-Class Business Correspondence* [M]. Linclonwood: NTC/Contemporary Publishing Group Inc.

Bucknall, Keven. 1999. *Chinese Business Etiquette and Culture* [M]. Raleigh: Boson Books.

Casperson, Dana May. 1999. *Power Etiquette* [M]. New York: AMACOM.

Carney, Marie. 1948. *Etiquette in Business* [M]. New York: McGraw-Hill Book Company, Inc.

Combs, Patrick. 2007. *Major in Success* [M]. Berkeley: Ten Speed Press.

Dresser Norine. 2005. *Multicultural Manners: Essential Rules of Etiquette for the 21st Century* [M]. Hoboken: John Wiley & Sons Inc.

Ehlich, Konrad & Wagner, Johannes. 1995. *The Discourse of Business Negotiation (Studies in Anthropological Linguistics)* [M]. New York: Mouton de Gruyter.

Genzberger, Christine. 1994. *China Business: The Portable Encyclopedia for Doing Business with China (World Trade Press Country Business Guides)* [M]. Petaluma: World Trade Press.

Ghauri, Pervez N. & Usunier, Jean-Claude. 2003. *International Business Negotiations, 2nd.Edition (International Business & Management)* [M]. Oxford: Pergamon Press

Harvard Business School Press. 2005. *Business Etiquette: The Results Drive Manager* [M]. Boston: Harvard Business School Press.

Hendon, Donald W., Hendon, Rebecca Angeles & Herbig, Paul A.. 1996. *Cross-Cultural Business Negotiations* [M]. Westport: Quorum Books.

Henney, Nella. 1922. *The Book of Business Etiquette* [M]. New York: Doubleday Page & Company.

Martin, Jeanette S. & Chaney, Lillian H.. 2006. *Global Business Etiquette: A Guide to International Communication and Customs* [M]. Westport: Praeger Publishers.

Maugham, W Somerset. 1977. *Cosmopolitans* [M]. Manchester: Ayer Company Publishers.

Post, Emily. 1923. *Etiquette* [M]. New York: Funk & Wagnalls Company.

Post, Peggy & Post, Peter. 2005. *The Etiquette Advantage in Business* [M]. New York: HarperCollins Publishers Inc.

Post, Peggy. 2004. *Emily Post's Etiquette* [M]. New York: HarperCollins Publishers

Inc.

Sabath, Ann Marie. 1997. *Business Etiquette In Brief* [M]. Cincinnati: Adams Media.

Varner, Iris & Beamer, Linda. 2006. *Intercultural Communication in the Global Workplace* [M]. Shanghai: Shanghai Foreign Language Education Press.

黄志颖,Phillip Bruce,Elfed Roberts.2006.商务英语沟通[M].上海:复旦大学出版社.

金正昆.2005.商务礼仪[M].北京:北京大学出版社.

林莹,毛永年.2006.西餐礼仪[M].北京:中央编译出版社.

李红,陈丹.2005.敢说礼仪英语[M].北京:机械工业出版社.

刘一平,李宏亮.2006.商务英语口语[M].北京:北京大学出版社.

Pellegrine, Thomas R..2005.谈判英语一日通[M].张中倩,译.北京:科学出版社.

曲继华.2003.丝巾风情[M].北京:中国轻工业出版社.

师晟.2004.领带结戴和选配[M].上海:东华大学出版社.

王大伟.2005.新视野大学英语视听说教程第三册[M].北京:外语教学与研究出版社.

徐小贞,白莉,吴芳.2005.国际商务交际[M].北京:高等教育出版社.

杨俊峰.2000-2001.国际商务礼仪[讲座].大连:大连外国语学院.

杨文慧,周瑞琪.2003.商务礼仪英语[M].广州:中山大学出版社.

余慕鸿,章汝雯,曹霞,何宁生.2005.商务英语谈判[M].北京:外语教学与研究出版社.

张燕彬.2001.国际商务礼仪[M].沈阳:辽宁教育出版社.

周文柏.1992.中国礼仪大辞典[M].北京:中国人民大学出版社.

庄恩平,庄恩忠,姚海芳,赵明.2004.跨文化商务沟通案例教程[M].上海:上海外语教育出版社

http://andrewferguson.net/tag/tie/

http://careerplanning.about.com/od/communication/a/email_etiquette.htm

http://careerplanning.about.com/od/officeetiquette/Office_Etiquette.htm

http://careerplanning.about.com/od/workplacesurvival/tp/cell_phone.htm

http://careers.asp.radford.edu/Resumes/FaxEmailEtiquette.pdf

http://en.wikipedia.org/wiki/Etiquette#Western_business_etiquette

http://icandressmyself.blogspot.com/2008/08/business-per-usual.html

http://jobsearchtech.about.com/od/letters/l/bl_block_p.htm

http://jobsearchtech.about.com/od/letters/l/bl_mblock_p.htm

http://jobsearchtech.about.com/od/letters/l/bl_sblock_p.htm

http://life.familyeducation.com/eating-out/etiquette/48924.html

http://owl.english.purdue.edu/owl/resource/653/01/

http://propr.ca/2009/presentation-etiquette-its-about-the-participants-not-the-speaker/

http://triedandtrueministries.blogspot.com/2010/04/titanic-he-knows-who-he-is.html

http://webcache.googleusercontent.com/search?q =cache:ZSx33lgS_NoJ:www.chinesecuisines.net/dinner.html +Dining +etiquette +varies +with +the +character +and +

purpose +of +a +banquet +and +in +different +areas&cd =1&hl =en&ct =clnk&client = firefox−a

http://www.associatedcontent.com/article/692853/ how_to_properly_use_the_dining_table.html?cat=22

http://wenda.tianya.cn/wenda/thread?tid=7a665db9f4471b16

http://www.a−to−z−of−manners−and−etiquette.com/index.html

http://www.brooksbrothers.com/scarfknots/scarfknots.tem

http://www.brooksbrothers.com/tieknots/tieknots.tem

http://www.businesstravelogue.com/businessGifts.html

http://www.crummer.rollins.edu/career_management/skills/letters.PDF

http://www.cyborlink.com/

http://www.ehow.com/articles_2105−workplace−etiquette.html

http://www.ehow.com/how_2053579_have−appropriate−handshake.html

http://www.ehow.com/video_4990683_give−persuasive−presentation.html

http://www.emilypost.com/index.htm

http://www.etiquette−school.com/didyouknow.php

http://www.etiquette−school.com/pastandpresent.php

http://www.etweb.fju.edu.tw/business/fjweb/course_metirial/letter/format.html

http://www.faxesanywhere.com/fax_etiquette.asp

http://www.io.com/~hcexres/textbook/genlett.html#

http://www.missouriwestern.edu/CareerDevelopment/pdf/buscorr.pdf

http://www.odu.edu/~kdepew/GCPs05.ppt

http://www.outreach.washington.edu/elp/sample/ebusN140_01c_05.asp

http://www.pasadenaisd.org/rayburn/clubs/bpa/contest/businesscorrespondence.html

http://www.sasked.gov.sk.ca/branches/elearning/ts1/resources/subject_area/ELA/ ELARR/Special_Forms_of_Writing.shtml

http://www.savvy−business−correspondence.com/IndentedBizLetter.html

http://www.savvy −business −correspondence.com/TypesBusinessCorrespondence. html

http://www.silkcharm.com

http://www.silkcharm.com/ban1_example.htm

http://www.silkcharm.com/long3_example.htm

http://www.tabletalk.org/tipsonmanners.htm

http://www.tasaram.com/tying−basic.html

http://www.tie−a−tie.net/bowtie.html

http://www.tie−a−tie.net/fourinhand.html

http://www.tie−a−tie.net/halfwindsor.html

http://www.tie−a−tie.net/windsor.html

http://www.titanic−titanic.com/forum/viewtopic.php?f=8&t=4238

http://www.worketiquette.co.uk/giving−a−presentation.html

http://www.workshoppersonline.com/office_etiquette3e.htm

北京高等教育精品教材立项项目

英语国家概况

　　《英语国家概况》是大学英语提高阶段的通选课教材，采用电子教程光盘与纸质版教材相结合的编写模式，配套使用。

1. 纸质版教材：供课堂教学使用，内容包括美国、加拿大、英国、爱尔兰、澳大利亚和新西兰等英语六国概况，任课教师可根据教学要求和学生情况对上述国家进行选择性教学。

2. 电子教程光盘：电子教程光盘供拓展学习使用，内容更加丰富，为课堂教学内容的拓展与延伸，包含大量精美插图和音视频教学资料；涵盖六大部分内容，分为美国、加拿大、英国、爱尔兰、澳大利亚、新西兰，以及新加坡、南非和印度等九国的概况，分为十八章进行介绍。

3. 配套习题：有各类练习题七百余道。每节附练习题 10 题(Section Exercises)，习题型式包括正误判断、多项选择和连线等客观题型；每章后附综合练习题 15-20 题(Chapter Exercises)，主要形式为填空、短语解释和简答等主观题型。练习题部分的设计可为学生通过四、六级考试和研究生英语入学考试提供帮助。

纸质版书号：978-7-301-13847-2

纸质版定价：32.00 元

总主编：史宝辉

主编：訾缨

向授课老师赠送《电子教程》。

北京大学出版社

北京市海淀区成府路 205 号
北京大学出版社外语编辑部
邮政编码：100871
电子邮箱：zbing@pup.pku.edu.cn

邮购部电话：010-62752015
市场营销部电话：010-62750672
外语编辑部电话：010-62765217　010-62767315

《国际商务礼仪英文教程》

尊敬的老师：

　　您好！

　　为了方便您更好地使用本教材，获得最佳教学效果，我们特向使用该书作为教材的教师赠送本教材配套参考资料。如有需要，请完整填写"教师联系表"并加盖所在单位系(院)公章，免费向出版社索取。

北京大学出版社

教 师 联 系 表

教材名称	《国际商务礼仪英文教程》		
姓名：	性别：	职务：	职称：
E-mail:	联系电话：	邮政编码：	
供职学校：		所在院系：	(章)
学校地址：			
教学科目与年级：		班级人数：	
通信地址：			

　　填写完毕后，请将此表邮寄给我们，我们将为您免费寄送本教材配套资料，谢谢！

北京市海淀区成府路 205 号
北京大学出版社外语编辑部　李颖
邮政编码：100871
电子邮箱：evalee1770@sina.com

邮 购 部 电 话：010-62534449
市场营销部电话：010-62750672
外语编辑部电话：010-62767315